Silent Power

The Discreet Formula for Global Influence and Control

Mia Galgau

Silent Power

How to build silent strength through anonymous structures, low-visibility positioning, and sovereign-level intelligence

A strategic manual for private individuals, entrepreneurs, investors, and diplomats

Introduction to Silent Power

In a time when visibility is mistaken for strength, a small number of people have discovered something else: real power moves quietly. It doesn't rely on recognition or applause. It grows in restraint, in distance, and in the ability to shape outcomes without leaving fingerprints.

Silent Power is not about hiding. It is about knowing how to be present without being exposed, how to hold control without noise, how to influence across borders without giving up privacy. These pages reveal the discreet setups used by investors, family offices, founders, and sovereign thinkers who value resilience more than recognition and continuity more than spectacle.

You will not find recycled theories here, or motivational slogans dressed as wisdom. What you will find is a disciplined method—an architecture built from law, structure, and discretion. It will show you how to own assets without becoming their public front, how to run companies without being reduced to a line in a registry, how to expand influence without becoming a magnet for compliance or curiosity. You will learn how to reduce the digital trails and legal traps that capture most people automatically, and how to place your identity, wealth, and movement inside systems that guard rather than expose.

The ground is solid. Every idea rests on tested legal bases, intelligence-grade methods, and cross-border case practice. This book offers clarity, not speculation—practical insight into how silent influence actually works in wealth, in business, and in life.

Whether you are an investor who values privacy, a professional weary of exposure, or someone determined to build sovereignty in a world that insists on disclosure, this book is more than reading material. It is a manual for invisible command, a roadmap for those who prefer to remain the author of their design rather than the subject of someone else's record.

Read it once. Apply it with discipline. Keep it for life

Power That Doesn't Announce Itself

In an age addicted to exposure, performance, and endless disclosure, discretion has become an act of defiance. Modern systems—legal, financial, and digital—are built to track, catalog, and display. Success is expected to be loud. Wealth must be exhibited. Strategy must be explained. Yet enduring power does not operate under those rules.

True power does not announce itself.

This book presents another architecture of influence—one that works without spectacle, without noise, without leaning on fragile validation. It is not about disappearing. It is about governing. Not escaping the system, but moving above it through design.

Silent Power gives founders, investors, advisors, and decision-makers a practical framework for acting without exposure. It rests on the principle that visibility is not the same as value, and that often the most strategic presence is the one that leaves no mark.

The foundations come from more than twenty years of legal and structural work across jurisdictions, assets, and governance. These pages reflect practices used by family offices, entrepreneurs, public figures, and sovereign professionals who sought not only to protect wealth but also to keep control over their own autonomy.

This is not a collection of tricks. It does not bend or ignore the law. Every tool described is grounded in legality, compliance, and discipline.

But law and structure are only the start. In today's environment, survival requires more.

Discipline in what is spoken—and what is left unsaid. Discipline in when to appear—and when to remain upstream. Discipline in which jurisdictions to trust—and when to leave them.

This book is not a replacement for professional counsel. It is a companion for those who already know that complexity cannot be avoided, but exposure can. Laws evolve. Treaties shift. Jurisdictions change. Power, if it is to last, must be reviewed, adapted, and designed again and again.

Silent Power is not about silence for its own sake. It is about silence as leverage. It is about sovereignty that does not look for recognition—but still commands it.

Let others chase attention. Let others overshare and perform. You build what lasts. And when the design is finished, only you will know where the true entrance stands.

About the Author

Mia Galgau is a lawyer and strategic advisor with nearly two decades of experience guiding private individuals, executives, investors and public actors across multiple jurisdictions.

Her work focuses on the intersection between law, mobility, reputation, and power — particularly in environments where visibility becomes risk and discretion becomes structure.

Throughout her career, she has supported clients in delicate transitions, cross-border restructurings, private disputes, diplomatic contexts, strategic relocations and high-pressure situations where the cost of error is structural rather than symbolic.

Her writing reflects the philosophy that underlies her professional practice: clarity over noise, legality as protection, structure as freedom, and sovereignty as a disciplined way of living.

She publishes under the Taxhells Strategic Series, a collection dedicated to bringing coherence to complex global lives.

Also by Mia Galgau

HNWI Survival Manual Enhanced Edition - When Your Wealth Becomes A Target. *A Strategic Operating System for High Net Worth Individuals*

This expanded edition is written for people whose lives have entered a phase where visibility becomes leverage, where privacy is currency, and where structure matters more than effort. More than a guide, it functions as a practical operating system for those who must remain coherent under pressure — whether the pressure comes from litigation, politics, reputation, emotional fracture, or institutional scrutiny.

This edition goes deeper than the original: it connects exposure with strategy, explains how risk moves across jurisdictions, and shows how to build a life that does not collapse when circumstances shift. Readers learn how to protect assets without appearing defensive, how to maintain influence without noise, and how to design legal, personal and psychological architectures that continue functioning even when they step away.

Written for HNWIs, family principals, diplomats, entrepreneurs and discreet decision-makers, it offers something most people in these positions never receive: understanding, structure and the tools to replace improvisation with sovereignty.

Nomad Structures - Design Your Life - How to build a global life without breaking it. *A Legal and Strategic Framework for Mobility Without Instability*

Many books celebrate freedom across borders; very few explain what it takes to sustain it without legal, emotional or financial damage. Nomad Structures is a practical guide for people who want to live globally without becoming vulnerable to tax conflicts, compliance failures, banking barriers, relational instability or geopolitical friction.

It teaches how residence, domicile, citizenship, banking, property, relationships and emotional discipline interact, and how to design mobility in a way that is both legally stable and personally sustainable. Readers learn to avoid mistakes that ruin the "digital nomad dream," and instead build a coherent structure they can live inside, not merely travel through.

This book is for founders, investors, diplomats, mobile professionals, and anyone who refuses to choose between freedom and order. It transforms mobility from an escape into a strategic architecture — one that protects, sustains and evolves with the individual.

The Gatekeeper – Strategic foundations for diplomats, operators and political elites. *A Manual for Those Who Navigate Power Without Being Consumed by It*

Most books speak about influence from the outside; The Gatekeeper addresses those already inside or on the threshold of environments where perception governs outcomes and silence is negotiation.

It reveals how political, diplomatic and elite systems actually behave – where incentives originate, how agendas collide, and why being technically competent is not enough to survive the internal pressure of these spaces.

The book teaches how to build authority without signaling aggression, how to avoid being manipulated by institutional players, and how to preserve identity, reputation and coherence in rooms where information is currency.

It is a handbook for diplomats, advisors, intermediaries, public figures, and private actors who find themselves adjacent to power structures that can elevate or destroy them.

Above all, it is written for people who must understand the logic behind influence – not to perform, but to survive it.

INDEX

Chapter I – Introduction: What is Silent Power? * The Difference Between Influence and Visibility * Why Silent Power Matters in Today's World * Hypothetical Models of Invisible Empires * The Nominee Investor with Global Holdings * The Cultural Patron Operating Through Foundations * The Cross-border Political Strategist * Closing Note – Legality and Ethics of Silent Power

Chapter II – Foundations of Strategic Discretion * The Psychological Roots of Strategic Discretion * A Different Relationship with Attention * Risk Perception and Information Control * Emotional Detachment from Visibility * Silence as Leverage: Strategic Non-Exposure in Action * Information Asymmetry: Saying Less, Controlling More * Structural Distance: Owning Without Exposure * Silence as a Negotiation Framework * Reputation as a Passive Asset * Digital Discipline: Maintaining Discretion in an Age of Surveillance * Understanding What Exposes You * Digital Infrastructure as an Asset or a Liability * Operational Separation: Building Firewalls Between Roles * Jurisdiction Matters: Where Your Data Lives * Legal Visibility vs Real Exposure * Legal Visibility is Not Absolute * Strategic Use of Public Registers * Designing for Control Without Visibility * Jurisdictional Arbitrage and Exposure Mapping * Asset Placement and Silent Mobility * Principles of Strategic Asset Placement * Real Estate Ownership Without Personal Exposure * Silent Holdings in Art, Gold, and Tangible Assets * Mobile Assets Without Triggering Residency * Financial Instruments and Private Equity Access * Silent Branding: How to Build Influence Without Visibility * Presence Without Personhood * Strategic Voice, Not Personal Story * Controlled Appearances and Selective Presence * From Founders to Ghost Founders: Letting the Brand Speak * Global Navigation Strategy: Jurisdictions, Residency and Access Without Exposure * Residency ≠ Control, Presence ≠ Exposure * The Role of Jurisdictions in Silent Power * Mobility as a Strategic Asset * Legal Presence Without Personal Risk * Sovereign Logic: Living by Design, Not by Default * Final Note – Strategic Discretion Requires Personal Architecture

Chapter III – Structuring Control Without Exposure * Principles of Control Without Ownership * Control Is a Function, Not a Status * Separation of Functions for Legal Protection * Control Through Architecture, Not Authority * Nominee Structures and Fiduciary Roles * Definition of a Nominee and Fiduciary Role * Lawful Uses of Nominee Arrangements * Elements of a Secure and Effective Nominee Agreement * Ethical and Compliance Considerations * Foundations, Trusts and Hybrid Entities * Private Foundations: Ownership Without Owners * Trusts: The Anglo-Saxon Standard of Invisible Control * Hybrid Entities: Mixing Corporate and Fiduciary Logic * Control Through Design, Not Possession * Power of Attorney and Delegated Signatures * Understanding the Power of Attorney as an Instrument of Silent Operation * Delegated Signature vs. Formal Position * * Limits, Risks and Legal Validity * The Signature as a Tool of Presence Without Exposure * Multi-Jurisdictional Governance * Jurisdiction Shopping Is Not Tax Evasion * Why Legal Dispersion Reduces Strategic Risk * Strategic Layering: Control, Registration, and Enforcement * Compliance and Coordination * Private Agreements vs Public Records * The Legal Force of Private Contracts * The

Limitations of Public Records * Designing the Interface Between Private and Public * Risk Management and Evidence * Selecting the Right People for Visible and Delegated Roles * Trust Is Not Enough: Profile, Background and Compatibility * Written Agreements Are Mandatory * Choosing Institutional vs. Private Fiduciaries * Contingency Planning: Replacing, Monitoring, and Exiting * Building Resilient Systems of Power * Autonomy Through Internal Rules and Triggers * Long-Term Legal Validity * Human Succession and Knowledge Transfer * Enduring Power Is Invisible, Not Absent * Final Note - Control Is Not About Ego, But Design

CHAPTER IV - The Art of Invisible Living * Designing a Lifestyle That Doesn't Attract Noise * The Myth of Luxury Visibility * Wealth Signaling vs. Wealth Shielding * Choosing Environments That Reinforce Discretion * Mobility Without Trace: Smart Travel and Residency * Second Residencies and Visa-Free Corridors * Digital Footprints While Moving Across Borders * When and Where to Declare (or Not Declare) Presence * Discreet Communication and Digital Hygiene * Devices, Metadata, and the Illusion of Privacy * Clean Channels for Sensitive Discussions * Behavioral Patterns That Reveal More Than Data * Managing Wealth Without Flash * How the Ultra-Wealthy Operate Quietly * Financial Habits of Discreet Families * Leveraging Private Banks Without Attracting Attention * Networks, Relationships, and Strategic Silence * Building Influence Without Building Noise * When to Speak, and When Silence Is the True Signal * The Role of Trusted Intermediaries * Living Authentically Without Leaving Traces * Purpose Without Performance * Legacy Over Lifestyle * Peace as the Ultimate Asset * Final Reflection: Privacy is Power, But Only if Lived Consistently

CHAPTER V - Digital Silence: Cyber Hygiene for the Elite * Introduction: Why Silent Power Requires Digital Precision * What Actually Exposes You Online * The Myth of Content Security * Platforms That Incriminate Without Warning * Exposure Through Devices, Not Decisions * Behavioral Leakage: The Invisible Exposure * Corporate Infrastructure and Email Traceability * Domain Names and WHOIS Exposure * Email Systems: Traceability, Metadata and Correlation Risk * Cloud Platforms and Collateral Traceability * Aligning Infrastructure with Jurisdictional Logic * Digital Tools for Secure Operations * Communication Tools: Messaging Without Trace * Secure Browsing and Access: Where and How You Connect * File Management and Document Security * Passwords, Access and Digital Succession * Designing Multi-Layered Cyber Discretion * Segregation of Roles and Identities * Layered Jurisdictional Mapping * Operational Compartmentalization * Silent Audits and Digital Simulations * The Role of Continuous Cyber Discipline * Discretion as a Daily Practice * The Cost of Inconsistency * Training and Alignment of Close Collaborators * Updating the Architecture: Strategic Maintenance * Final Note - Digital Discretion Is a Living System

CHAPTER VI - Legal Visibility vs Real Exposure * * Introduction: Seeing Is Not Knowing * What Regulators Can and Cannot See * Layers of Legal Visibility: Shareholders, UBOs, and Functional Roles * Jurisdictional Asymmetry in Disclosure Requirements * Delayed vs. Real-Time Reporting: The Window of Control * Legal

Obligations vs. Investigatory Access * Strategic Use of Public Registers * What Public Records Actually Reveal—And What They Don't * Using Buffer Roles, Nominee Appointments, and Visible Fronts * Managing Substance Declarations and Formal Responsibilities * How to Comply Without Exposing Command * Designing for Control Without Exposure * Legal Distance Through Structure: Ownership vs. Control * Proxy Voting, Silent Mandates, and Layered Governance * Invisible Steering: How Real Influence Operates Under Formality * Jurisdictional Layering as a Risk Management Framework * Visibility Thresholds and Legal Arbitrage * How "Significant Influence" Is Defined Differently Across Systems * Playing Below Thresholds: 25%, 10%, and Silent Capital * Cross-Referencing Across Systems: How Exposure Can Propagate * Designing Legal Presence to Resist Triangulation * The Role of Documentation and Narrative * Aligning Public Disclosures with Internal Agreements * Writing the Story That Your Records Will Tell * Managing Inconsistencies Between Filings and Control * Preparing for Audits, Inquiries, and Legal Mapping * Final Note – Visibility Is a Tool, Not a Threat

CHAPTER VII - Asset Placement and Silent Mobility * Introduction: Ownership Is Not Power—Placement Is * Strategic Real Estate Ownership Without Personal Exposure * Why Direct Ownership Creates Visibility and Risk * Holding Real Estate Through Layered Legal Vehicles * Leaseback, Usufruct, and Decoupled Enjoyment * Navigating Land Registries, Tax Triggers, and Local Compliance * Silent Holdings in Art, Gold, and Tangible Assets * The Appeal of Non-Financial, Mobile Assets * Storage in Freeports and Bonded Warehouses * Legal Custody vs. Economic Control * Documentation, Insurance, and Discreet Liquidation * Private Equity, Funds, and Non-Listed Investments * Participating Without Public Trace * Using SPF, SICAV, LP, or Fund-of-Fund Structures * Exercising Influence Through Side Letters and Capital Mandates * Timing, Exit Strategies, and Jurisdictional Filters * Mobile Assets: Yachts, Jets, and Vehicles of Influence * Holding Through SPVs or Leasing Structures * Avoiding Residency, Customs, and Registry Risks * Mobility Without Nexus: Using Flags, Ports, and Agreements * Documentation, Crew Management, and Silent Operations * Liquidity, Cash Equivalents, and Financial Placement * Banking Without Attribution * Jurisdictional Distribution of Liquid Assets * Nominee Accounts, Silent Signatories, and Layered Mandates * Managing Reporting Obligations Under FATCA and CRS

CHAPTER VIII - Silent Branding (For Founders & Leaders) * Introduction: Presence Without Performance * Presence Without Personhood * Strategic Voice, Not Personal Story * Controlled Appearances and Selective Presence * From Founders to Ghost Founders * Final Note – Let the Brand Speak: But Not for You

CHAPTER IX - Global Navigation Strategy * Introduction: Borders Are Not Barriers—They Are Tools * Residency ≠ Control, Presence ≠ Exposure * The Strategic Separation of Legal Ties * Understanding How Presence Creates Unintended Consequences * Designing Movement Without Triggering Jurisdictional Obligations * The Value of Administrative Disconnection * The Role of Jurisdictions in Silent Power * Why Not All Jurisdictions Serve the Same Function * Using Complementary Systems for Holding, Managing, and Protecting * Risk Dispersion Through Legal Incompatibility

* Timing, Entry Points, and Layered Operations * Mobility as a Strategic Asset * Moving Without Establishing Nexus * Time Thresholds, 183-Day Rules, and Center-of-Life Presumptions * Strategic Relocation and Reputational Management * Negotiated Residence and Pre-Immigration Tax Planning * Legal Presence Without Personal Risk * Structuring Access Without Attachment * Director Roles, Licenses, and Authorized Representation * Remote Governance and Virtual Command * Decoupling Signature from Liability * Sovereign Logic: Living by Design, Not by Default * Choosing Your Legal Environment Intentionally * Lifestyle, Infrastructure, and Legal Autonomy * Resilience Through Jurisdictional Diversification * Navigating the Transition from Citizen to Strategist * Final Note – To Belong Everywhere Is to Be Owned Nowhere

CHAPTER X – The Final Layer: Silence as Leverage * Introduction: Silence Is Not Absence—It Is Command * The Asymmetry of Information Flow * Why Silence Increases Perceived Value * Managing Timing and Access to Information * Creating Uncertainty to Control Tempo * Delayed Disclosure and Tactical Ambiguity * Withholding Clarity as Negotiation Tool * Structuring Communications to Protect Optionality * When Not Answering Is the Most Powerful Answer * Controlling Narrative Without Being Its Source * Letting the Brand Speak Without Personal Exposure * Orchestrating Perception Through Proxies * Using Silence to Invite Strategic Assumptions * Non-Reactivity as a Form of Domination * Breaking the Cycle of Provocation and Response * Emotional Neutrality in High-Stakes Environments * Turning Silence into Psychological Weight * The Discipline of the Unsaid * Legal Silence: What Not to Put in Writing * Strategic Silence: When to Vanish from a Process * Ritual Silence: As Identity, Not Tactic * Final Note – Power That Speaks Is Power That Can Be Interpreted

Closing Words

CHAPTER I - INTRODUCTION: WHAT IS SILENT POWER?

In Today's World of Exposure

In today's climate, visibility is too often mistaken for value, and noise for influence. Social platforms treat attention as currency, corporations confuse publicity with credibility, and wealth is increasingly paraded instead of preserved. Yet the kind of power that lasts—effective, stable, and respected—has always operated in silence.

Silent Power is the ability to influence, protect, and expand across borders without being seen, tracked, or dependent on recognition. It is not secrecy for its own sake, nor unlawful concealment. It is a deliberate position, chosen by those who understand that strength grows in restraint and that leadership begins with sovereignty.

This form of power does not live on likes, followers, or rankings. It is built on structure, discipline, and discretion. The dynasties that endure—whether family offices, investment networks, or cultural legacies—rarely occupy headlines. Yet they move capital, shape policy, and drive innovation with quiet precision.

This book does not offer shortcuts or fashionable tricks. It provides a framework for remaining in control without holding visible title, for building and operating companies discreetly, for reducing exposure across registries, media, and digital trails, and for designing systems across jurisdictions that grant freedom without demanding visibility. It shows how to act globally while remaining privately resilient.

The aim is not to escape responsibility. It is to safeguard autonomy, protect reputation, and preserve leverage in a world eager to consume identity. Whether you are a founder ready to step back from the spotlight, a private investor seeking durable structures, or a global operator pursuing sovereignty, this book will help you strengthen your ability to act without being seen.

Silent Power is not about vanishing. It is about operating beyond reach.

The Difference Between Influence and Visibility

One of the great illusions of our time is the confusion between being seen and being powerful. In a world run by algorithms, the loudest voice captures the widest audience, and those with the largest following are mistaken for the most influential. Corporations measure relevance by media appearances, institutions chase rankings, and individuals stage their lives as if exposure itself proved worth. This perception is not only false—it is strategically dangerous.

Visibility is not influence. Visibility is exposure.

Influence operates whether or not anyone is watching. It is the capacity to shape outcomes, redirect flows of capital, set the terms of negotiation, or shift the tone of a room without standing at the podium. Someone constantly in the spotlight may appear powerful, but if their presence is not backed by access, design, and control, their authority evaporates once the cameras switch off. By contrast, an individual unknown to the public can move billions across borders, steer policy decisions, or determine the course of industries with a single instruction.

The distinction lies in the mechanics. Visibility is reactive, dependent on attention, sentiment, and moods that shift overnight. Influence is structural, embedded in systems of ownership, legal layers, contractual obligations, jurisdictional choices, and networks of trust that outlast headlines. Visibility makes you subject to narrative. Influence allows you to design the frame within which narratives unfold.

This distinction matters because visibility is a trap. The more visible you are, the more your actions are constrained by expectation and surveillance. Public figures are constantly monitored, their decisions filtered through reputational risk, every move dissected by commentary or regulatory scrutiny. Exposure magnifies vulnerability: legal disputes, digital leaks, reputational attacks, or betrayals all become sharper under the spotlight. Influence, by contrast, thrives in opacity. It works best when the mechanics of decision and control are hidden behind layers that deflect attention.

Silent Power is built on this principle. It is not about absence, but about design. True power is structured, not displayed. It is cultivated through careful choices: arranging entities so that control does not equal ownership, setting operational flows that obscure who directs them, managing communication so messages land where intended without leaving a public trail, and resisting the temptation to mistake visibility for validation.

To practice Silent Power requires self-restraint and clarity of purpose. It means recognizing that exposure is not proof of strength but a mark of vulnerability. It means constructing systems where influence runs through proxies, intermediaries, and layered jurisdictions rather than personal display. It means learning to control without seeking credit, to design without demanding recognition, and to act decisively while remaining outside the frame.

This book is not a manual of tricks or evasions. It is not about hiding in shadows or cultivating paranoia. It is about mastery—of structure, of jurisdiction, of communication. It is about becoming the architect rather than the spokesperson, the strategist rather than the spectacle. Those who see the difference between influence and visibility are not only better protected; they are the ones who, in time, shape the world without appearing to touch it.

Why Silent Power Matters in Today's World

The twenty-first century has produced a paradox that defines our time. Never have individuals been so visible, searchable, and connected—and never have they been so vulnerable to surveillance, interpretation, and exploitation. Every digital step leaves a trail. Every transaction creates a record. Every network maps connections that can be read, copied, and used. In this environment, exposure is no longer an accident; it is the default state of modern life.

The systems that organize daily existence—corporate registries, tax transparency regimes, compliance protocols, social platforms, and now artificial intelligence—were not designed to protect privacy. They were built to extract, categorize, and monitor. Metadata has become identity. A person is increasingly defined not by character or intent, but by the data points, affiliations, and signals that machines collect and process.

Against this backdrop, Silent Power is not a luxury. It is sovereignty. It represents the ability to protect what matters most: time, reputation, leverage, and freedom. Without it, wealth becomes a beacon for unwanted attention, reputation turns into hostage to algorithms, and freedom erodes under the weight of compliance and exposure.

Why does this matter? Because visible wealth does not only invite admiration. It attracts scrutiny, envy, and opportunistic attack. Because digital behavior is treated as evidence, available not only to governments but to competitors, adversaries, and the public at large. Because reputation is no longer confined to local circles; it is algorithmic and global, shaped by systems that translate a single action in one country into consequences across many others.

Those who operate internationally without discretion face a multiplying problem: they are exposed in several legal systems at once. What begins as a disclosure in one jurisdiction may trigger compliance demands in another. A statement posted online may damage reputation in markets far from its origin. Cross-border taxation, overlapping regulation, and legal presumptions now follow visibility rather than intent.

Silent Power provides another way. It allows ownership without constant display, leadership without public affirmation, and influence that crosses borders without turning its bearer into a target. It makes it possible to build networks and act effectively while preserving autonomy from systems designed to categorize and control.

This is not concealment. It is design. Silent Power is the deliberate configuration of presence so that it serves personal and strategic goals, rather than being dictated by outside agendas. It is a method of reasserting control in a world determined to interpret every move.

Hypothetical Models of Invisible Empires

To see Silent Power in practice, it helps to look at how it takes shape in real structures. The following models are not depictions of any one individual, but composites drawn from strategies that appear repeatedly in international finance, family offices, and global networks of influence. They show how wealth and authority can be exercised without exposure, and how architecture—rather than visibility—becomes the true source of resilience.

The Nominee Investor with Global Holdings

Picture an investor based in Central Europe whose modest public profile hides a far greater reach. Their portfolio spans commercial real estate, private equity, and venture capital on three continents. Yet on paper their presence is barely detectable. Their name does not appear in company registries, shareholder lists, or land records. Even determined searches by regulators, journalists, or rivals reveal little more than a professional shell.

The invisibility comes from design. In jurisdictions like Luxembourg and the Netherlands, holding companies are layered in neutral but strategic ways. Fiduciary directors—professionals who lend their names in exchange for fees—handle the signatures and formal decisions. To an outsider, these directors appear to be in charge.

Behind that facade, binding resolutions and proxy agreements quietly channel decision-making power back to the investor. Private mandates ensure that voting rights flow through them, not through the names on the documents. In practice, they control the levers while leaving no fingerprints.

Publicly, the investor is tied only to a small advisory firm, a company that owns no assets and generates no headlines. This modest identity explains their existence without revealing their empire.

The model illustrates the essence of Silent Power. It does not erase presence but redirects it. By separating identity from ownership, the investor reduces legal exposure, reputational risk, and personal vulnerability. If one jurisdiction changes its rules, the structure shifts. If a fiduciary is compromised, a replacement takes their place. The system endures because it is layered, modular, and impersonal.

To the outside world, this investor seems cautious, even ordinary. In reality, they move capital and opportunity across borders, always beyond reach, always outside the spotlight.

The Cultural Patron Operating Through Foundations

Now consider a discreet family in Switzerland that has shaped culture for more than twenty years. Their support extends to museums, concert halls, scholarships, and public initiatives across Europe, Asia, and Latin America. Their influence is unmistakable, yet their name never appears in press releases, annual reports, or donor walls. To the public they are absent. To insiders, they are central.

At the core is a Liechtenstein umbrella foundation, chosen for its confidentiality and flexible governance. From there, funds flow through vehicles in the Cayman Islands and New Zealand–jurisdictions recognized for strong philanthropic frameworks and regulatory resilience. These entities act as grantors and intermediaries, ensuring compliance locally while distancing the family from beneficiaries.

Externally, the grants seem to come from generically named foundations with independent boards and professional trustees. Internally, the family steers strategy through private charters and reserved powers embedded in foundation statutes. They decide which institutions expand, which fade, and which values persist—all without signing public documents or appearing at ceremonies.

The design is deliberate. It protects narrative control. By remaining "strategic contributors" instead of visible benefactors, the family avoids solicitation by opportunists, reputational damage if projects fail, or scrutiny from regulators who might link philanthropy to wealth management. Their giving is surgical, their presence hidden behind structures that draw attention to programs rather than patrons.

The paradox is striking: cultural institutions celebrate anonymous support, while behind the curtain a private family shapes agendas and nurtures networks. Their influence endures because it is invisible; their reputation remains intact because it is silent.

This model shows that even in philanthropy—perhaps especially in philanthropy—visibility can be a liability. By giving through layers of structures, the family preserves autonomy, safeguards reputation, and influences culture without stepping into the spotlight.

The Cross-Border Political Strategist

Consider an international legal advisor in Europe, someone whose official profile looks far smaller than their actual reach. They hold no public office. Their name does not appear in diplomatic directories or government rosters. To the public they are invisible. Yet in private they shape decisions that alter national destinies.

Their reputation rests not on publicity but on discretion, built over decades. In West Africa, where institutions are fragile and transitions uncertain, they are trusted by heads of state, ministers, and reform committees. They are called not to give speeches, but to address problems too sensitive for public view: revising constitutions, restructuring elections, mediating disputes, or negotiating with supranational lenders whose conditions determine a country's budget.

On paper, the advisor's role is modest: consulting contracts, advisory boards, technical reports. These documents confirm activity but never reflect real authority. Their influence flows instead through private referrals and quiet mandates. Each mission is temporary on its face, yet over time these calls have made the advisor a structural actor in several governments.

Their strength rests on three choices: trust, neutrality, and distance. By never seeking office, they avoid the suspicion of rivals. By working through supranational contracts, they maintain the look of impartial expertise. By limiting visibility to technical fields, they shield themselves from political cost.

To those in power, their role is invaluable. To the public, they do not exist. This absence is design, not weakness. It lets them mediate reforms without becoming a target, steer negotiations without being tied to elections, and shape constitutions without public baggage.

This case captures a central truth of Silent Power: influence does not require titles or ceremony. Sometimes the strongest position is outside the frame—recognized by insiders, unseen by outsiders. By combining law, jurisdiction, and discretion, the strategist shows how presence can be undeniable and untraceable at once.

Closing Note - Legality and Ethics of Silent Power

It is important to stress that the principles in this book are not designed to cover misconduct. Silent Power is not a tool for deception or a shield for unlawful activity. It is a discipline of design—structuring life, assets, and influence to preserve autonomy while staying within the law.

The strategies described rest on legitimate foundations: corporate frameworks recognized globally, fiduciary practices accepted across jurisdictions, and governance models that are public, lawful, and enforceable. They do not promote fraud, misrepresentation, or evasion. They reflect conscious use of discretion, jurisdictional awareness, and structural foresight. Silent Power is about operating intelligently, not recklessly; deliberately, not by improvisation.

In an age when visibility has become a commodity and exposure a systemic risk, reclaiming privacy is not dishonesty—it is responsibility. Living without constant observation is not secrecy; it is balance. Designing presence deliberately restores the dignity of sovereignty in a world that rewards endless transparency yet punishes it without mercy.

These insights must not be twisted for illicit concealment or manipulation. Silent Power is not about avoidance; it is about stability. It equips you to preserve wealth, influence, and identity in ways that are lawful, compliant, and durable. Those who practice it are not escaping responsibility—they are reclaiming control of their narrative.

In that sense, Silent Power is more than strategy. It is a philosophy: influence without noise, freedom without exposure, structures that endure precisely because they do not rely on being seen.

It is about living with clarity, intention, and sovereignty in a world that confuses visibility with security.

CHAPTER II - FOUNDATIONS OF STRATEGIC DISCRETION

We Live in an Age of Performed Legitimacy

Visibility today is treated as proof of worth. To be seen is assumed to be credible. To be silent is assumed irrelevant. Digital platforms, institutions, and even governments reinforce this belief every day. Yet the assumption is false. Visibility does not create value–it exposes it. And exposure, once magnified by global systems, is never neutral. It invites attention, interpretation, and intervention.

For those who move capital across borders, manage sensitive assets, or cultivate lasting influence, discretion is no longer a matter of taste. It is not simply a personal preference or a mark of refinement. In the twenty-first century, discretion has become a strategic necessity.

Discretion as Structure, Not Silence

Once, discretion meant diplomacy, refinement, or restraint. A discreet person knew when not to speak, when to hold back, when moderation itself was the sign of character. That world is gone. Today, discretion has to be engineered. It cannot rest on polite silence or refusal of the spotlight. It has to be built into systems–legal, digital, and operational–that absorb attention away from the source of control.

Silent Power grows out of discretion. But not all discretion produces power. Many people remain unseen out of fear, lack of opportunity, or simple preference. They are obscure, but they hold no leverage. Strategic discretion is different. It is intentional. It is both a mindset and an infrastructure, designed to reduce exposure, preserve control, and move influence beyond reach.

The Three Dimensions of Strategic Discretion

What separates strategic discretion from mere quietness are three qualities.

First, it is active, not passive. Strategic discretion is not about avoiding interviews or staying off social media. It is about actively shaping what is said, what is published, and what is perceived. It curates the points of contact between reality and perception. The discreet actor does not vanish; they redirect. The world sees what has been prepared for view, not what actually governs.

Second, it is systemic, not occasional. A single encrypted call or a temporary pseudonym cannot shield a life that is otherwise exposed. True discretion is woven through legal setups, financial layers, digital discipline, and reputational posture. Once exposure happens, it cannot be undone. Systems must be in place before the moment of need.

Third, it is sovereign, not defensive. Discretion is not fear. It is choice. The discreet individual decides when and how to appear, which parts of their presence are projected, and which remain inaccessible. They are not hiding; they are selecting. In that selection lies sovereignty—the ability to set the terms of engagement rather than receive them.

Why Strategic Discretion Matters Now

The need for discretion has always been present, but the cost of exposure has never been higher. A scandal once reached a handful of papers. Today it circles the globe in hours. A document filed is not only archived; it is indexed, digitized, and searchable. An image shared is not only seen; it is copied, stored, and cross-referenced.

Visibility is not neutral. Platforms monetize it. Adversaries weaponize it. Courts and tax authorities treat it as evidence. Every trace becomes taxable, investigable, or contestable. In this environment, the most powerful are not the loudest. They are those who design systems that outsiders cannot easily read.

The Internal and External Dimensions of Discretion

Strategic discretion has two fronts: the inner discipline of the person, and the external design of their systems.

Internally, it requires a different psychology. Those who master silence think differently. They care less about being acknowledged and more about being effective. They know that noise consumes energy, while silence preserves it. Restraint is not passivity—it is focus.

Externally, discretion becomes functional leverage. Silence strengthens negotiation: the side that speaks least holds the stronger hand. In ownership, discretion separates control from legal title, keeping assets active without attaching them to a single name. In positioning, discretion builds mystique, deters attack, and shields intent until the time to act arrives.

The digital dimension is decisive. Modern exposure is rarely voluntary. It hides in metadata, communications, clouds, and registries.

Emails, location pings, bank transfers, filings—all combine into a shadow biography, readable by others even if the individual has said nothing. Strategic discretion means taking control of those fragments before they form a story you did not write.

The Core Principle

At the center of strategic discretion lies one rule: build systems that speak less than you do. In practice, that means creating legal, financial, and operational frameworks that project only the minimum signal required. The world should see coherent activity, but not the forces that matter most—control, intent, decision-making. Those remain hidden in structures designed for durability.

Discretion as Sovereignty

Strategic discretion is not a retreat into obscurity. It is not the denial of presence. It is the luxury of choice—the ability to appear when necessary and to withdraw when it serves better. It transforms invisibility into strength, making a position unassailable precisely because it cannot be mapped. More than anything, it is sovereignty.

The goal is not to disappear. Disappearance is defensive. The goal is to become unreadable, so that the systems built to monitor and expose never capture what matters. In that unreadability lies endurance. In that discipline lies Silent Power.

The Psychological Roots of Strategic Discretion

The decision to remain discreet is never just tactical. It is not a trick for avoiding attention or a temporary response to circumstance. At its foundation, discretion is psychological—a way of relating to the world that shapes every choice, every risk assessment, every exchange. To understand Silent Power, you must understand the inner discipline that sustains it.

Most people are trained early to crave recognition. Applause, validation, visibility—these are treated as proof of value. Students are praised, professionals ranked, celebrities admired. Visibility becomes addictive because it confirms existence. Without it, many feel irrelevant.

Those who cultivate Silent Power think differently. Their sense of self is not tethered to outside mirrors. Their freedom matters more than attention. Success is not measured in recognition but in sovereignty. They are energized not by being seen but by being unencumbered—free to act without interference, free to build without noise, free to decide without distortion.

The difference is profound. It is a psychological reconfiguration: separating identity from visibility. Where others feel diminished when unseen, the discreet feel protected. Where others collapse without acknowledgment, the discreet thrive in silence. Their satisfaction comes from clarity of purpose and mastery of structure, not from applause.

They often share three traits:

- A high tolerance for solitude. They do not fear absence from networks or headlines. Solitude is not exclusion but insulation—a condition that preserves clarity and autonomy.
- Emotional containment. They resist provocation and the lure of attention. Every reaction is disclosure, and by mastering the impulse to respond they maintain control.

- A long horizon. Immediate recognition holds little weight compared to lasting outcomes. They trade applause today for stability tomorrow.

At the core is self-containment. They do not outsource validation. They know that influence is measured not in noise but in continuity. Their restraint is not weakness; it is architecture.

In this way, psychology and strategy converge. The mind that resists the temptation of visibility is the same mind that designs systems to remain beyond reach. Silent Power is not imposed. It begins within—discipline of thought before discipline of structure.

A Different Relationship with Attention

Attention has become a universal currency. Those who dominate headlines and feeds are celebrated as winners of visibility. Their names circulate, their faces repeat, their presence seems constant. But attention carries a cost. Every moment in the spotlight is purchased with scrutiny, vulnerability, and obligation.

The discreet recognize this early. They do not avoid attention because they lack ambition, but because they understand its price. To attract attention is to invite oversight. To invite oversight is to surrender privacy. And once privacy is gone, autonomy erodes.

For most, recognition feels intoxicating. A headline, an interview, an invitation to a panel creates the illusion of progress. But the discreet evaluate these differently. Every appearance is not just exposure—it is a test of structure. The question is never, *"Will this make me visible?"* but *"Does this strengthen or weaken the architecture I have built?"*

The calculus is different. To the majority, visibility is a reward. To the discreet, it is a liability, tolerated only when justified by lasting gains. They weigh disclosures with questions most never consider: Does this reveal mechanisms better left unseen? Will it bind me to narratives that limit future options? Does the short-term validation outweigh the long-term cost in leverage?

This posture is not anxious hesitation. It is deliberate. They know every contact creates a trace, and every trace can be reassembled into a map. Protecting operational integrity is more important than enjoying applause.

By treating attention this way, they do not vanish. They become unreadable. Their appearances are curated, their absences strategic. To outsiders, this may look enigmatic. In reality, it is design. Attention is rationed and deployed only when it reinforces sovereignty.

In a culture addicted to exposure, this restraint looks radical. But it is liberation. By refusing to trade autonomy for applause, the discreet secure something more valuable than attention itself: the freedom to act without being consumed by the gaze of others.

Risk Perception and Information Control

A defining trait of those who master discretion is their sensitivity to risk. Information is never neutral. Every disclosure carries weight, every signal can be amplified, distorted, or weaponized once released. What others treat as casual sharing, they treat as strategic exposure. This is not paranoia—it is realism. Once something is visible, it cannot be undone.

For them, discretion is not secrecy. Secrecy suggests hiding, which implies weakness. What they practice is control—intentional management of information flow. They decide who knows what, when, and on what terms. Nothing is casual. Each fragment is released only when it serves strategic value. By managing this flow, they create privacy and leverage at once.

This mindset often comes from experience. Founders who have endured reputational attacks know how a stray comment can cost investors. Cross-border investors know how a disclosure in one country can trigger audits in another. Diplomats and lawyers know that silence is often the strongest negotiating tool. Clients of private banks and family offices know that discretion is not luxury but survival.

For all of them, discretion builds a perimeter of control. It is not just personal privacy; it is defense of assets, relationships, and influence. The line is not drawn with walls but with discipline: the discipline to limit disclosure, to compartmentalize, to treat every interaction as a potential risk vector.

To outsiders, this may look excessive. To those under constant visibility, it is necessity. They know risk is not distributed evenly. The wealthy and the visible carry disproportionate exposure—their mistakes magnified, their signals read with more scrutiny. Recognizing this asymmetry is what separates those who lose control from those who remain sovereign.

In this sense, information control is not withdrawal. It is design. By managing what leaves their sphere, they control how others interpret them, how adversaries approach, how institutions respond. What looks like silence is narrative management. What looks like absence is sovereignty.

Emotional Detachment from Visibility

One of the most striking traits of those who practice strategic discretion is their indifference to recognition. In cultures obsessed with status symbols, rankings, and cycles of attention, this detachment can seem unnatural. Yet for the discreet strategist it is the natural result of looking beyond the spectacle. While others spend their energy trying to be noticed, they spend theirs shaping outcomes. Where most chase applause, they focus on effectiveness.

They do not measure success in headlines or follower counts. Their satisfaction lies in continuity: in seeing systems adjust quietly to their intent, in watching structures endure, in knowing that control remains intact without explanation. Recognition is not proof, and it is not prize. To them, it is distraction.

This detachment shows in practice. They decline prestigious roles without anxiety. Their ego does not demand proximity to the stage, because they know the real levers of power are rarely visible. They are comfortable working through proxies or institutions without feeling diminished, understanding that invisibility extends reach. They can withstand long periods of obscurity without resentment, confident that results speak louder than appearances.

This posture is not humility in the usual sense. It is not modesty or avoidance of praise. It is a discipline sharpened by deliberate choice. It is the ability to step away from public noise without losing private command. In fact, it is often the most ambitious who gain most from this detachment, because it protects their drive from the corrosion of constant exposure.

Discretion, in this sense, is not the opposite of ambition. It is ambition refined. It strips away the vanity of recognition and channels energy into structures, results, and legacies that last. In hostile and saturated environments, where visibility breeds vulnerability, this refinement marks the line between fleeting prominence and lasting influence.

Silence as Leverage

Silence is one of the most misunderstood behaviors. Popular culture treats it as weakness or passivity. Training manuals reduce it to a pause in negotiation, a trick to pressure the other side. In the architecture of strategic discretion, silence is none of these things. It is not hesitation. It is leverage.

Leverage is the ability to shape outcomes without direct force. It shifts balance without overt confrontation. Silent Power applies this principle by creating asymmetries—of information, of visibility, of perceived risk. The less you reveal, the more others must assume. In that uncertainty lies advantage.

In negotiation, the party that speaks least often sets the pace. Words, once spoken, become commitments; silence preserves options. Every disclosure narrows the field; silence leaves it open. Those who rush to explain or justify weaken themselves. The discreet strategist resists. They know silence compels others to project, to guess, to overcommit. Each word withheld becomes a form of pressure—calm, invisible, stronger than argument.

Beyond negotiation, silence separates control from attribution. Those absent from registries, contracts, or publicity cannot be targeted easily. In public life, silence disarms critics, depriving them of material to exploit. In digital systems, silence limits exposure, reducing data that can be indexed or weaponized.

This is not retreat but design. Silence maintains control of timing. It dictates when and how information enters the system. It ensures disclosure happens on one's own terms. In this sense, silence is not emptiness. It is architecture—an invisible framework shaping behavior around it.

The discreet strategist does not seek silence for silence's sake. They use it with precision, knowing that absence can speak louder than words. Silence signals restraint, control, and confidence. It is the difference between reacting and governing. In the world of discretion, silence is not lack of power. It is power, distilled.

Information Asymmetry: Saying Less, Controlling More

In every negotiation, transaction, or alliance, power tilts toward the side that reveals least. Strategic silence is not absence of speech but a choice: to withhold position, structure, or intent, forcing the other party to act on assumptions. The less you disclose, the more they fill the gaps—and projections are rarely accurate.

This is information asymmetry. Whoever says less, controls more. Every disclosure is a window into your architecture. It signals resources, constraints, objectives. To the untrained, disclosure feels like strength. To the discreet, every disclosure is a cost. Once released, information cannot be retrieved. What begins as explanation can later be used as evidence, leverage, or narrative against you.

In high finance, the principle is ritual. In mergers and acquisitions, the side that avoids over-explaining its valuation or weaknesses often secures the advantage. By leaving elements undefined, they force counterparts to speculate, overbid, or reveal more in due diligence. The asymmetry arises not from deception but restraint. The one who knows more and says less shapes the deal.

Family offices apply the same rule through structure. Entities are layered across jurisdictions, ownership separated from control, mandates dispersed. Even if one piece leaks, it reveals nothing of the whole. Privacy is preserved not by secrecy but by asymmetry—outsiders see fragments, never the design.

In diplomacy, silence adds another layer. To speak too much is to show need or urgency. The diplomat who holds back often forces others to reveal priorities, make concessions, or overextend. Silence becomes a signal of strength.

The lesson is simple: those who reveal less observe more. In high-stakes arenas, the side with fewer public statements, fewer documents, less noise holds flexibility. They can adapt without contradiction, renegotiate without embarrassment, withdraw without cost. Their silence preserves options. The verbose trap themselves in their own record.

Strategic discretion is not about hoarding information. It is about calibrating its release so that each disclosure serves purpose and every silence maintains leverage. Saying less does not mean contributing less.

It means controlling more—because control belongs to those who govern the flow of information, not to those who surrender it.

Structural Distance: Owning Without Exposure

One of the most effective forms of silent leverage lies in separating ownership, control, and appearance. To the untrained eye, these roles seem inseparable: the one who owns must also control, and the one who controls must inevitably appear. For those who practice Silent Power, resilience begins when that chain is broken—when distance is designed so that no single role reveals the whole.

This distance is not just legal maneuvering. It is structural in every sense: legal, operational, reputational, and relational. It reflects an understanding that visibility is never distributed evenly, and whoever stands closest to the surface carries the greatest exposure. By design, the true strategist never occupies that position.

Take a trust holding shares in a holding company. On paper, the trust is the owner, its fiduciaries and administrators listed in registries. Yet the individual who drives the strategy may never appear as settlor or beneficiary. Instead, they operate quietly as protector, advisor, or architect—always present, never exposed.

Or consider a corporate setup where a director signs contracts, attends meetings, and communicates with regulators and press. Every action is shaped by private instructions and powers of attorney. The director carries visibility; the principal retains control.

Foundations often serve a similar role. A foundation can manage grants, investments, or philanthropy under its own name, governed by independent trustees and statutes. The benefactor's identity may be recorded in private instruments but never enters public reports. To the outside world, the entity acts in its own right; the individual behind it remains unseen.

These arrangements are not mere shields. They are instruments of leverage. They allow the true decision-maker to operate free from the constant pressure of regulators, journalists, or adversaries. Negotiations take place from a position of autonomy. Inquiries and challenges meet layers of structure before reaching the core. Each layer absorbs pressure, deflects risk, and protects the strategist.

When designed carefully, structural distance turns exposure into insulation. Regulators may demand documents from a trustee, but the trustee knows little. A journalist may name a director, but the trail stops there. A partner may contest a decision, but the authority they confront is delegated. The architecture ensures that the seat of control is always steps removed from external reach.

The deeper the insulation, the greater the freedom. Decisions are made without fear of disclosure, negotiations proceed without reputational pressure, and wealth remains sovereign because it is not tied to visible roles. What looks fragmented to outsiders is, in truth, coherence by design: a system where the visible absorbs exposure and the invisible holds power.

Silence as a Negotiation Framework

In elite negotiations, silence is never a void. It is a deliberate signal. To those who understand it, silence does not suggest hesitation or lack of preparation. It communicates independence. It conveys that the silent party is not bound to the outcome, that they are ready to walk away, that their alternatives are strong enough to make urgency unnecessary.

This dynamic shifts psychology. The side that stays silent pushes the other into reaction. When one speaks less, the other fills the gap with explanations, justifications, or concessions. In doing so, they reveal doubts, priorities, or urgency that would otherwise stay hidden. Silence becomes the anchor of the dialogue, forcing the counterpart to interpret signals and give more.

The principle is clear in private equity and corporate deals. When an investor avoids overexplaining valuation or rushing into disclosures, they project strength. The other side, uncertain of real limits, may raise offers or concede terms just to reduce ambiguity. Silence shapes both the numbers and the psychology behind them.

The same applies to conflict resolution. Shareholders in dispute, or states in delicate talks, often find that the side speaking least sets the rhythm. Silence here is not disengagement but control of tempo. By withholding immediate reaction, the discreet negotiator compels the other side to show their hand.

Even in technical areas—asset repatriation, tax negotiations—when done within the law, the same logic applies. The party that resists early over-disclosure preserves flexibility. By holding details until the right moment, they prevent regulators or adversaries from dictating the narrative.

Strategic silence is not absence. It is presence without vulnerability. It is the conscious choice to reveal only when disclosure reinforces position. It is the ability to decide not just what to say, but when, where, and under what conditions. Jurisdiction, language, and forum become instruments of control, carefully chosen so that words are interpreted on one's own terms.

In this framework, silence is not passive. It is architecture—an element of design that strengthens negotiation by ensuring control rests with the party disciplined enough to say less.

Reputation as a Passive Asset

Among the many forms of leverage that come with Silent Power, reputational silence is perhaps the least understood. In a culture where visibility is equated with relevance, not having a loud digital footprint or a history of public exposure is often seen as weakness. In practice, it is the opposite. In an age where nearly every action is documented, indexed, and archived, absence itself has become rare—and therefore valuable.

The individual whose name does not trigger headlines, whose digital presence is minimal, and whose record carries no speculation enjoys a kind of freedom that visible figures no longer have. They can enter sensitive environments without bias, baggage, or political interpretation. A discreet investor at a negotiation table, a private advisor in a diplomatic mission, or a candidate for a board seat unknown to search engines often holds greater room to maneuver than a well-publicized figure whose persona has already been dissected.

Private bankers prefer clients unburdened by scandal. Diplomats trust interlocutors who carry no political weight of their own. Boards often prefer the strategist who stays out of headlines to the celebrity whose every action is under scrutiny. In these spaces, reputation is not measured by presence but by absence—the absence of noise, controversy, and overexposure.

Reputational silence is a blank slate. Without trails or visible affiliations, the discreet strategist can move in multiple directions. They negotiate without being constrained by history, propose without being limited by past statements, and operate across jurisdictions without reputational chains imposed by others. Silence creates optionality, and optionality is leverage.

This state does not arise by chance. It is cultivated. It is the result of deliberate choices: limiting appearances, avoiding unnecessary commentary, compartmentalizing personal and professional lives, and building structures that project function without revealing identity. The real leverage comes not from constant assertion but from the discipline of withholding—legally, intentionally, consistently.

In a world tuned to respond to noise, silence itself becomes a signal. It shapes perception without offering material to weaponize. While the visible scramble to manage narratives, the silent dictate the terms of engagement by leaving no narrative to attack. The paradox is clear: in a culture obsessed with attention, the strongest power belongs not to those who shout, but to those who never step onto the stage. Reputational silence is not emptiness. It is currency, valued precisely because so few can maintain it.

Digital Discipline: Maintaining Discretion in an Age of Surveillance

In the analog world, discretion could be preserved with restraint in lifestyle, careful correspondence, and selective appearances. Records were scattered and hard to link. That world is gone. Today, every device, platform, and transaction produces data. Every search query, location ping, or financial transfer leaves a permanent trace stored in systems you do not control.

Modern discretion cannot rest on behavior alone. It has to be engineered. Digital discretion is not about vanishing from the grid. It is about designing presence so that what is recorded, if recorded at all, is strategically neutral or aligned with your chosen narrative. The goal is not disappearance—it is containment.

Most underestimate the challenge. Entrepreneurs and high-net-worth individuals often assume discretion means declining interviews or avoiding social media. In truth, the deeper risks come from overlooked details: metadata in email attachments, automatic cloud backups, behavioral patterns logged by phones, geolocation tags embedded in casual photos.

The discreet strategist understands that every digital act is a disclosure. A message sent, a flight booked, a document signed electronically—all generate trails readable by governments, corporations, or private intelligence. The question is no longer *"How do I stay invisible?"* but *"How do I make what is visible work in my favor?"*

Discipline here means compartmentalization. Personal communications separate from professional. Sensitive activities segmented across platforms, devices, and jurisdictions. Financial flows routed through systems built for resilience, not convenience. Even choices about what not to record or store become part of the design. Silence in the digital age is not lack of activity, but absence of exploitable traces.

For those managing wealth, influence, or reputation across borders, this discipline is non-negotiable. Without it, discretion collapses under the weight of data others can interpret and exploit. With it, silence regains its force—not as retreat, but as deliberate design.

True Silent Power today begins not in parliaments or boardrooms, but in the infrastructure of devices, networks, and communications. Discretion has migrated from conduct to systems. To master it is to realize that in an age of surveillance, control comes not from speaking less, but from deciding what your silence leaves behind.

Understanding What Exposes You

For most, the word "exposure" suggests scandal: leaked documents, a sudden headline, a public storm. In reality, exposure in the digital era is quieter. It comes from ordinary actions that leave unintended traces.

Registering a domain name under your real identity may seem harmless until years later it links back to a project you no longer control. Using the same email for personal and professional correspondence creates a thread mapping your entire network. Sending a PDF can disclose metadata about your device and the exact time it was created.

Cloud storage is another silent vulnerability. By storing data under jurisdictions with weak protections or broad surveillance laws, you surrender control over your records. Even trivial choices—accepting cookies on a financial app or allowing location access on a phone—feed streams of information that can be cross-referenced, sold, or subpoenaed.

A photograph offers similar risk. A casual upload may contain GPS coordinates, device IDs, and timestamps. To most, it is a snapshot. To those with tools and intent, it is a breadcrumb trail of your movements and environment.

Silent operators understand exposure does not begin with extraordinary mistakes. It begins with the defaults of modern systems. For them, discretion is not reactive but systemic. They design digital identity with layers: jurisdictional layers that separate one legal system from another; functional layers that distinguish personal from professional; reputational layers that keep the visible identity neutral while shielding the true center of control.

Discretion begins not with silence but with awareness. It demands the discipline to know which data points are exposed by default, the foresight to anticipate how they might connect, and the intelligence to build systems that minimize those signals. In the digital world, what exposes you is rarely what you say. It is what you forget you are saying without words.

Digital Infrastructure as Asset or Liability

In the digital age, infrastructure is never neutral. It either protects you or exposes you. The very tools that enable communication, trade, and administration also embed traces of identity and intent. Ignoring those traces is surrendering control. Designing them deliberately is reclaiming sovereignty.

Infrastructure as Strategy

Consider something as ordinary as a company's domain name. At first glance, it is just an internet address, a technical requirement for email and websites. Yet a simple WHOIS search can uncover ownership, billing details, and administrative contacts—data that regulators, journalists, or competitors can later index and exploit. What looks harmless is, in fact, a doorway into your architecture.

The same applies to email. A free Gmail account, scanned and stored under U.S. jurisdiction, may serve ordinary users well enough. For high-level operators, it is a channel of exposure: every message subject to access by legal or extralegal means. By contrast, a private server in Switzerland, Iceland, or another jurisdiction with strong privacy protections turns the same act of communication into sovereignty. Infrastructure determines whether you are silently observed or properly shielded.

Even documents carry risk beyond their words. A PDF may embed usernames, device IDs, timestamps, or company environments in its metadata. A contract prepared for negotiation can betray details about the sender that speak louder than the document itself.

Video calls are no different. Depending on the platform, a confidential meeting may travel through networks monitored by surveillance alliances, or through secure servers in neutral jurisdictions. Participants rarely notice the difference, yet infrastructure decides whether a call is private conversation or archived intelligence.

For the discreet, this is not paranoia. It is configuration. Digital discretion is achieved not by abandoning tools but by designing their use with precision. Domain registrations are handled offshore through trustees. Email accounts are segmented by jurisdiction and function. Devices operate outside mainstream cloud ecosystems. VPNs run on servers privately controlled, not consumer-grade applications. Each decision introduces distance between the individual and the trace left by their tools.

Every layer represents intent. Each choice signals whether the architecture was built for convenience, compliance, or discretion—or ideally, a balance of all three. Infrastructure itself becomes strategy. To ignore it is to build a fortress with open gates. To master it is to turn ordinary tools into shields of sovereignty.

Operational Separation: Firewalls Between Roles

One of the most underestimated practices of digital discretion is the separation of roles. Most people live as a single, unified identity: one email for work and personal matters, one phone for business and family, one calendar blending board meetings with private dinners. It feels efficient. It is also dangerous. Every overlap creates patterns. Every pattern becomes a map that others can read.

Strategic operators understand that discretion requires decoupling. Their roles as investors, advisors, family members, or public figures cannot collapse into a single fingerprint. Each role stands on its own, with its own systems and perimeter. This is not concealment—it is design. It ensures information from one sphere does not bleed into another, creating avoidable vulnerabilities.

The practice starts with infrastructure. Devices are separated: one phone for negotiations, another for family, a third for travel. Computers follow the same discipline, with no overlap of accounts, passwords, or applications. Even IP addresses are assigned to specific entities so that traffic cannot be correlated across environments.

Calendars, contacts, and cloud systems apply the same rule. A board member should not appear in the same database as a family doctor. Strategic planning documents should not live in the same storage as personal correspondence. Each sphere has its own container, and those containers remain apart—not just in appearance but in architecture.

Communication follows the same pattern. Sensitive exchanges, especially across jurisdictions, are encrypted and routed through controlled systems. The aim is not to dodge compliance but to keep deliberations insulated from casual chatter or operational logistics.

Without operational separation, even the most careful individual is exposed. Patterns emerge naturally, allowing outsiders to connect dots that were never meant to align. A shared login, a single overlapping email, or a device used across roles can collapse an entire structure into transparency. Efficiency becomes exposure.

The essence of operational separation is not secrecy but control of inference. By building firewalls between roles, the strategist prevents outsiders from drawing conclusions that compromise sovereignty. Each role appears coherent on its own terms, but the links between them are broken. What remains is a structure in which influence moves freely while identity stays contained.

In the architecture of Silent Power, operational separation is not optional. It is the discipline that keeps every layer of life—personal, professional, strategic—distinct, resilient, and beyond reach.

Jurisdiction Matters: Where Your Data Lives

One of the most overlooked dimensions of digital discretion is jurisdiction. Where exactly is your data stored? Under which laws does it fall? Which courts can demand access, and under what treaties can that access be shared across borders? These questions, rarely asked by ordinary users, determine whether your digital infrastructure protects you—or exposes you.

To many, the cloud is just "the cloud," a vague space where files are stored. In reality, data is always physical. It sits on servers in specific territories, subject to the authority of specific governments. Hosting strategic archives on a U.S. platform, regardless of encryption or marketing claims, places them squarely within the reach of U.S. courts, intelligence agencies, and cross-border cooperation agreements. Confidentiality is not just about technology. It is about law.

Discreet operators know this. They treat the jurisdiction of their data as carefully as the jurisdiction of their companies or their tax residence. Just as one would not casually incorporate a holding company in a hostile environment, one should not casually host records in a territory where privacy is routinely subordinated to state or corporate power.

For that reason, high-level operators often select infrastructures aligned with discretion. Switzerland, with its long tradition of neutrality and strong legal protections, remains a favored base for secure services. Liechtenstein and Luxembourg, though small, offer mail and storage providers backed by robust privacy frameworks. Nordic countries, strict in governance yet protective of personal privacy, are increasingly popular for encrypted solutions. Outside Europe, neutral or non-aligned jurisdictions with clear commitments to data sovereignty also attract those who want protection from geopolitical pressure.

The lesson is straightforward: data stored in the wrong jurisdiction can undermine even the strongest legal structure. A family office may build trusts, foundations, and layered entities to protect assets, yet if its records sit in a surveillance-heavy jurisdiction, those protections can collapse with a single request. Structure must extend to storage. Architecture must remain consistent across legal and technological layers.

In an era of systemic surveillance, digital discretion is no longer optional. It is the technological side of Silent Power. And like every other layer—legal, financial, operational—it must be designed, monitored, and updated with discipline. Visibility may be cheap. Discretion requires investment: in infrastructure, in legal counsel, in constant vigilance.

Legal Visibility vs. Real Exposure

Transparency rules, public registers, and compliance systems make it easy to believe privacy no longer exists. Companies must disclose. Bank accounts are reported. Beneficial owners are registered. The illusion is that discretion has been eliminated, that everything is visible, and therefore Silent Power is impossible.

That belief is misleading. Privacy has not disappeared—it has changed.

There is a difference between being legally visible and being truly exposed. Registers and filings create a formal layer of visibility, but that does not automatically translate into strategic vulnerability. The existence of data in a database does not mean it is public, accessible, or damaging. Conversely, invisibility on paper does not guarantee safety if daily operations constantly reveal patterns elsewhere.

Not all visibility creates risk. A public record of incorporation may be required, but it does not have to show who makes decisions, how the entity is financed, or what strategies it pursues. A beneficial ownership register may exist, but access may be limited to regulators, not journalists or competitors. Well-designed disclosures can satisfy the law while protecting discretion.

Nor does every disclosure equal exposure. Listing a director's name or a shareholder's percentage may fulfill compliance while revealing little of substance—especially if structures are layered. A single visible node in a network does not compromise the whole when what lies behind it is shielded. The strategist knows discretion is not about erasing every trace, but about deciding which traces exist and under what conditions.

Equally important: invisibility does not imply wrongdoing, and legality does not require publicity. The assumption that being unseen is evidence of misconduct is one of the most damaging myths of modern discourse. Silence is not crime. Discretion is not deception. The law requires certain disclosures, but it does not demand more. To remain silent outside those obligations is not avoidance. It is sovereignty.

The strategist therefore does not fight every disclosure, nor surrender to the idea that transparency must equal exposure. Instead, they map carefully where legal visibility begins and ends, ensuring what becomes visible is neutral while what matters most stays protected.

In a world that confuses visibility with legitimacy, this distinction is leverage. Silent Power is not about rejecting law or resisting compliance. It is about making sure that what the law reveals does not compromise what must remain untouchable.

Legal Visibility Is Not Absolute

Legal visibility refers to disclosures required under national frameworks: corporate registries, tax filings, compliance reports. These typically include shareholder details, ultimate beneficial ownership (UBO), and compliance with CRS, FATCA, or AML regimes. At first glance, such obligations suggest that discretion has no room left.

Yet legal visibility is neither absolute nor uniform. It varies by jurisdiction, entity type, and regulatory threshold. Many countries use a 25% UBO threshold, leaving smaller holdings unreported. Others exempt foundations or trusts from public visibility, limiting access to regulators only. The difference between a Liechtenstein foundation, a UK partnership, and a Luxembourg holding company is not superficial—it creates entirely different landscapes of visibility.

Legal visibility is also rarely immediate. Reporting cycles follow annual or quarterly timetables, which means disclosures are always slightly outdated. This delay creates a buffer, giving strategists time to adjust before information becomes official. Visibility is also fragmented. One authority holds shareholder data, another tax data, another compliance records. These systems often fail to integrate, and only someone with both access and expertise can reconstruct the whole picture.

Even when information is legally visible, access is restricted. In many jurisdictions, registries are limited to regulators, auditors, or investigative bodies. Journalists and competitors often cannot reach the most sensitive data. Legal visibility is filtered, and that filter is decisive in determining whether information is merely procedural or strategically dangerous.

The strategist recognizes this. The goal is not to evade compliance but to reduce functional visibility—visibility to actors who could weaponize it. A family office, for example, may comply fully with FATCA and CRS, yet design its structures so that the disclosed data is segmented across entities and jurisdictions, preventing outsiders from assembling a full profile.

The principle is simple: compliance and discretion can coexist. Proper design makes transparency a formality, not a vulnerability. Regulators see what they must. Others see nothing of consequence.

When structures are deliberate, transparency does not weaken sovereignty. It reinforces it. Silent Power thrives in this distinction—the ability to honor the law without surrendering the privacy that makes strategy possible.

Strategic Use of Public Registers

Public registers are often dismissed as nothing more than liabilities—mechanisms that strip away privacy and make discretion seem impossible. Yet when used deliberately, they can become part of the design. Registers reflect compliance, but they also create a stage where perception is managed and the deeper architecture remains untouched.

What appears in a register is never the whole story. A record shows what the law requires, not the true extent of control. With careful choices, disclosure can meet formal obligations while leaving sovereignty intact. Fiduciary directors or corporate nominees may be listed openly, while real authority flows quietly through private mandates or proxy agreements. To outsiders, the structure looks orderly and complete. To those who built it, the register is just the surface.

Minority stakes offer another example. A shareholder listed at ten or twenty percent may seem irrelevant, yet governance rights or contractual arrangements outside the register give them decisive influence. The filing satisfies the law, but leverage is preserved elsewhere.

In practice, many operators set up visible, compliant entities while anchoring true ownership in jurisdictions where details remain protected. A Luxembourg holding company may disclose every detail, but its ultimate owner sits inside a Liechtenstein foundation shielded from public view. Regulators have what they need; competitors and journalists do not.

The United Arab Emirates shows a similar pattern: free-zone companies operate legitimately and in full daylight, while underlying ownership is structured privately under rules that prevent public access. Switzerland takes yet another approach—compliance is delivered, but confidentiality remains. Regulators can see, the public cannot.

This is Silent Power applied to registers. It does not mean avoidance or deception. It means precision: providing what the law demands without offering more, making sure compliance does not turn into exposure.

Between the minimum required and the excess demanded by opportunists lies a space of sovereignty. The strategist occupies that space intentionally, disclosing what must be shown while guarding the rest. Silent Power does not ignore registers. It shapes them into instruments of control rather than instruments of surrender.

Designing for Control Without Visibility

At the center of Silent Power lies structural distance. The objective is not to vanish but to distribute presence across multiple layers, so that no single authority, registry, or jurisdiction ever holds the full picture. It is the practice of separating ownership from exposure, control from public view, compliance from vulnerability.

This separation does not rely on tricks. It relies on the disciplined use of familiar tools. A family business may be held by a company in one jurisdiction, managed by a trust in another, while strategy is directed by a board in a third. Each entity fulfills its obligations, filing reports as required. Yet no single regulator has the entire map. What is visible in one place remains incomplete without the pieces elsewhere.

The same applies to individuals. Real influence may be exercised through a power of attorney from a company they do not appear to own. A fiduciary director signs the contracts, while the principal remains behind the mandate. The name on paper is the delegate's; the sovereignty belongs to the unseen.

Foundations follow the same logic. A foundation may appear in public filings as the legal owner of assets. Yet letters of wishes, reserved powers, or protectors quietly steer those assets out of sight. The structure is compliant, but its strategic intent is private.

These techniques are not exotic. They are standard in private banking, estate planning, and international wealth preservation. What sets the discreet strategist apart is the way they combine them—layered across jurisdictions, synchronized across systems, each point of visibility incomplete on its own.

The value lies in separation. Structural distance allows full compliance with reporting regimes while ensuring that no individual appears as the direct controller of any single piece. More importantly, it prevents automatic associations. A holding in one country may seem neutral. An advisory role elsewhere may appear minor. Only when the fragments are connected does the true structure emerge—and unless due process compels it, that connection is never made.

In a world where banks, regulators, and digital systems increasingly integrate data, structural distance restores control. It is discretion built into the design itself. The discreet operator does not hide from visibility; they manage it so that no observation point ever shows the whole.

Silent Power is not about erasure. It is about redistribution. Not about secrecy, but about structure. Control endures while visibility is scattered, fragmented, and incomplete. And the key that ties it together remains with the strategist—never offered freely.

Jurisdictional Arbitrage and Exposure Mapping

A central pillar of Silent Power is the ability to chart exposure across jurisdictions. Every state plays by its own rules of disclosure, privacy, and reporting. What is freely accessible in one country may remain sealed in another. Data that is exchanged automatically under CRS or FATCA in one system may sit untouched in a jurisdiction outside those networks. For the strategist, these differences are not obstacles but instruments. By distributing ownership, management, banking, and personal presence across complementary systems, it becomes possible to remain compliant while keeping protection local.

Exposure mapping begins with precision. It means knowing exactly what each jurisdiction reveals, to whom, and under what circumstances. A company incorporated in one country may publish shareholder lists to the public. Another may limit disclosure to regulators, closing the door to outsiders. Some tax authorities push information directly into international exchange frameworks, while others keep it domestic. Privacy traditions vary just as widely—some states run surveillance cultures by default, while others embed confidentiality into law. By aligning each element of a structure with the jurisdiction that treats it most favorably, the operator makes sure that no single authority can assemble the full picture.

The approach gains real force when assets, management, banking, and residency are separated on purpose. Assets may sit in territories outside automatic exchange networks, so that ownership records do not circulate globally. Management can be exercised from jurisdictions with deep privacy traditions, shielding decision-making authority from casual inquiry. Banking may be structured apart from asset ownership, ensuring that the entity on an account is not the same one recorded as owner. Even personal presence—where one lives, works, or travels—can be designed so that residency does not automatically trigger taxation or regulatory claims.

This is not evasion. It is sovereign configuration. It rests on the recognition that compliance and discretion are not enemies. They can coexist if the architecture is deliberate. The goal is not to vanish, but to practice intelligent transparency: enough disclosure to meet the law, never so much that the individual becomes captive to systems of control.

Silent Power does not hide from legal obligations. It uses them. By understanding the reporting thresholds, the blind spots between jurisdictions, and the limits on access, it builds distance between the operator and the surface of operations. Regulators see what is accurate, but never the whole. The public sees what is coherent, but never final. Adversaries are left with fragments that remain unusable unless due process forces the connection.

This is the essence of exposure mapping. It does not resist visibility; it directs it. It does not avoid compliance; it shapes the consequences.

In the next section, we will move from mapping exposure to the placement of assets and mobility—what can be owned, where, and how, without triggering unnecessary disclosure or compromising sovereignty.

Asset Placement and Silent Mobility

Silent Power is expressed most clearly not in theory but in the practical design of how assets are held and moved. Ownership alone does not create sovereignty. Control comes from architecture, not title. And visibility does not always equal vulnerability—if the structure behind it has been built with intent.

Assets are more than property. They are nodes in a network of law, jurisdiction, and perception. The same house, company, or fund can either expose or protect its owner depending entirely on how it is placed. What matters is not simply *what* you own, but *where* you own it, *through whom*, and under which legal framework the relationship is defined.

Take real estate, often seen as the most exposed of assets. A property held in your personal name is a public declaration. It can be searched in registries, attached in litigation, or linked directly to you in tax filings. Place the same property inside a company or a foundation, and its visibility changes immediately. On paper, the asset belongs to an entity. Add layers—a trust in one jurisdiction holding a company in another—and visibility fragments further. Regulators may see pieces, but no single authority holds the entire map. Functionally, the property remains yours; in appearance, it does not.

Financial assets follow the same pattern. A bank account in personal name ties you directly to funds. Shift ownership to an entity or mandate, and distance is created. Even if one layer comes under scrutiny, the architecture prevents full exposure. Assets may be reported, but the decision-making pathways remain out of sight.

Mobility extends the principle. Moving assets across borders is not just logistics. It reshapes exposure. A portfolio shifted into another jurisdiction may trigger new reporting obligations—or bypass them. An operating company incorporated in one country but managed from another can change both its tax footprint and its visibility profile. Even personal presence matters: time spent in a country may be enough to establish residency, altering how assets are taxed or declared. Silent operators decouple movement from exposure, ensuring that presence does not automatically translate into liability.

Letters of wishes in foundations, private mandates in trusts, powers of attorney in holding companies—these are not arcane tools. They are standard instruments of private banking and wealth planning. What makes them powerful is the way they are combined. Used strategically, they allow assets to remain functional and compliant while insulating the individual from unnecessary exposure.

Silent Mobility means the ability to restructure without signaling weakness, to expand without triggering obligations, to move without leaving trails that others can weaponize. It does not evade existing systems; it configures them. Sovereignty is preserved because the architecture itself is sovereign.

Silent Power, in the end, is measured not only by what one can control but by what one can protect. Asset placement lays the foundation. Mobility ensures its endurance. Together, they form the operational dimension of discretion: the ability to act globally, lawfully, and strategically while staying beyond the easy grasp of visibility.

Principles of Strategic Asset Placement

Silent architecture does not appear by chance. It is the outcome of deliberate design, guided by principles that allow wealth to be preserved, enjoyed, and transferred without inviting unnecessary exposure. These principles are not exotic. They are recognized and practiced widely in private wealth management. What sets the discreet strategist apart is not the tools themselves, but the discipline with which they are applied.

First: separate legal title from beneficial control. The person who benefits from an asset need not hold it in their own name. Legal systems everywhere recognize vehicles that split ownership from use: trusts, foundations, nominee agreements, fiduciary mandates. By letting one entity hold title and another exercise control, the individual avoids being tied personally to every asset while retaining full function and benefit.

Second: fragment jurisdictions. Centralization is the enemy of discretion. Concentrating all assets, management, and records in one place guarantees visibility. Spread them across multiple legal systems, and no authority can reconstruct the whole. A company incorporated in one country, managed from another, and funded through accounts in a third creates a landscape where each authority sees part, but never all.

Third: place assets in favorable jurisdictions. Not every country participates equally in transparency regimes. Some retain confidentiality traditions. Others limit access to regulators only. Some apply thresholds that exempt certain holdings. Aligning each asset with the jurisdiction most favorable to its class ensures that disclosure obligations are met without opening unnecessary windows. This is not avoidance. It is configuration.

Fourth: use intermediaries with their own legal personality. Trusts, foundations, partnerships, and special-purpose vehicles are not inventions of secrecy. They are well-established in law. They provide distance between the individual and the asset, buffering wealth against liability, disputes, or opportunistic claims. A foundation may hold art, a trust may hold shares, a partnership may manage investments—each recognized, each compliant, each protective.

These principles appear daily in practice. Real estate is often held through companies, ensuring registries show entities, not individuals. Yachts and aircraft are registered under corporate vehicles in favorable jurisdictions, separating liability from personal use. Art and collectibles are stored in bonded warehouses or freeports, where contracts, not registries, define control. Private equity portfolios are routed through SPF companies, SICAV funds, or limited partnerships that combine governance, tax efficiency, and discretion.

What unites these practices is intent. They are designed not only for function, but for discretion. Structures ensure visibility is minimized, control is preserved, and protection is anchored in law rather than circumstance. Wealth continues to generate value while the individual remains shielded.

Silent Power is not about possession alone. It is about design. Wealth without structure is exposed. Structured wealth endures.

Real Estate Ownership Without Personal Exposure

Real estate is one of the most revealing asset classes. In many countries, land registries are public by default. Even where they are not, ownership triggers a cascade of filings—tax, municipal, insurance, compliance—that leave permanent traces. For someone who values discretion, personal title is one of the weakest positions to hold.

Silent operators resolve this by layering. Instead of purchasing directly, they acquire property through companies. A Spanish SL, a Swiss SA, or similar vehicles appear as the owners of record. To outsiders, the registry lists an entity. The individual remains invisible.

The shares of that entity are rarely held personally. They sit inside a holding company in a jurisdiction chosen for neutrality and favorable reporting rules. Even if the property company's name is searchable, the trail does not run straight back to the principal.

Management is also structured. Fiduciary directors may serve as the visible managers, handling contracts and compliance. Their authority, however, is tightly bound by private instructions. They act in public, but the principal directs in private.

Personal use of the property is equally intentional. The individual may hold a lease, a usufruct, or another contractual right from the owning entity. The arrangement is ordinary on paper, yet it provides full access without exposing ownership. To the registry, the property is corporate-owned and simply leased.

The result is balance. The property is compliant and usable, but the individual does not appear as owner in public records. What could otherwise become a target for lawsuits, reputational attacks, or opportunistic claims is insulated.

The principle is simple: visibility and control do not have to overlap. By separating legal title from personal identity, and by layering ownership, management, and use, the discreet strategist keeps both the asset and their sovereignty intact.

Real estate may be immovable, but exposure is not inevitable. With deliberate architecture, even the most visible asset class can become shielded, compliant, and discreet within a larger system.

Silent Holdings in Art, Gold, and Tangible Assets

Among the most discreet ways to preserve wealth are tangible assets—art, gold, luxury watches, rare collectibles, and similar stores of value. When structured correctly, they serve not only as alternative investments but as instruments of Silent Power. Their strength lies in portability, in independence from digital systems, and in the ability to layer and shield ownership. But discretion here does not come by default. It has to be designed.

The first principle is separation: ownership, custody, and attribution must never converge under the same name. A collector who buys a painting directly and registers it personally creates exposure, financial and reputational. The same work, held through a trust, a foundation, or an intermediary gallery, no longer points to the individual but to a legal entity. The art remains identical; the architecture around it is transformed.

Sophisticated operators rely on numbered storage accounts in freeports such as Geneva, Luxembourg, or Singapore. These facilities operate under customs control, offering fiscal neutrality and secure custody. Artworks, bullion, and collectibles can remain outside taxable circulation, stored indefinitely, traded between entities, or moved across jurisdictions—all within the discreet environment of customs. To the outside world, the asset exists. The owner does not.

Insurance and provenance records follow the same logic. Policies are issued in the name of the entity, not the beneficial owner. Certificates of authenticity and provenance are attached to the structure that holds title, whether a foundation, trust, or investment vehicle. If reviewed, the individual is absent. The asset is insured, authenticated, and tradable—without personal attribution.

Custody, ownership, and management are further split. One entity may hold title, another may manage insurance, another may arrange transport or valuation. No single channel reveals the full scope of ownership and control. The individual remains free to liquidate, move, or leverage the asset, yet their name never intersects with market-facing records.

From a tax perspective, tangible assets held in free circulation outside a person's country of residence often generate no reporting obligation until a sale or transfer occurs. This is why art, bullion, and collectibles function not only as stores of value but as silent vehicles of sovereignty. They exist beyond registries, without breaching compliance, and without unnecessary tax triggers.

Silent wealth is not hidden wealth. It is positioned wealth—placed beyond needless visibility. It is not secrecy but discretion: lawful, structured, and strategic. By separating ownership, custody, and attribution into distinct layers, the strategist keeps tangible assets valuable, functional, and liquid, yet protected from the vulnerabilities of exposure.

Mobile Assets Without Triggering Residency

Few forms of wealth combine prestige and vulnerability as clearly as mobile assets. Luxury vehicles, yachts, and aircraft project power, but they are also traceable. Unlike art in storage or bullion in a vault, these assets move. They cross borders, appear in ports, and interact with registries and regulators. Direct ownership, especially when tied to personal use, can create cascading liabilities: tax residency claims, customs duties, and intrusive compliance checks.

This is why seasoned operators rarely own such assets in their personal names. The absence of direct ownership is deliberate. The solution is layering. Mobile assets are placed in special purpose vehicles (SPVs) designed solely to hold and manage them. The SPV appears in registries, contracts, and insurance policies, while the individual remains outside the frame.

Access is secured contractually. The principal may use a yacht through a lease or a usage agreement with the SPV. The arrangement provides lawful enjoyment without personal liability. A jet may be owned by an offshore company, operated by a management firm, while the user appears only as a contractual beneficiary of the service. To regulators, the individual is a client, not an owner.

Jurisdictional choice is key. The country of registration for the SPV or the asset itself should not coincide with the user's tax residence. Otherwise, authorities may infer personal nexus and trigger residency rules. Neutral or specialized jurisdictions—Isle of Man for aircraft, Malta or Cayman for yachts, Luxembourg for vehicle SPVs—offer compliant yet protective environments.

Personal names must be absent from visible roles. Fiduciary directors or professional managers serve as public representatives, bound by private agreements that leave control with the principal. Public records show them, not the user.

When structured with discipline—clear documentation, contractual precision, and operational separation—these assets can be used fully and legally without becoming liabilities. Customs see valid registration. Tax authorities see compliant entities. What they do not see is a personal link that could establish residency or profile wealth.

Mobility does not have to equal exposure. A yacht can sail, a jet can fly, and a fleet of cars can operate without any of them turning into a trap. The difference lies not in the asset itself, but in the structure surrounding it. Separate ownership from use. Register carefully. With the right design, mobility becomes freedom.

Financial Instruments and Private Equity Access

Private markets—venture funds, private equity, bespoke debt instruments—offer some of the most effective frameworks for silent wealth. Unlike public securities, which leave visible trails through exchanges and filings, private markets are contractual and contained. For discreet investors, they provide access without publicity.

One key advantage is the absence of public registers. Shareholders or limited partners in private funds are known to managers, auditors, and regulators—not to the public. Presence is real, but exposure is limited.

Capital commitments are made through entities rather than individuals. A trust, foundation, or holding company subscribes to the fund, so the name on record is institutional. The investor receives returns while their personal identity remains shielded.

Distributions can also be routed strategically. Channeling profits through jurisdictions with favorable treaties ensures taxation where chosen, not where imposed. A Luxembourg or Dutch structure may unlock treaty advantages, while a Liechtenstein foundation or Singapore holding directs the flow discreetly.

Control does not require direct visibility. Voting rights or exit terms can be exercised through mandates, proxies, or contractual arrangements. The investor shapes outcomes without appearing in the room.

Handled properly, private equity offers the trifecta of Silent Power: compliance without exposure, taxation by choice, and insulation from litigation or media speculation. When disputes arise, it is the entity, not the individual, that appears. The architecture absorbs the pressure; the principal remains outside reach.

Silent mobility is not about hiding. It is about placing every asset where it is most effective, most protected, and least visible. A shareholding acquired without structure is a liability. The same shareholding, routed through entities and mandates, becomes an instrument of sovereignty.

Wealth can be counted. Silent wealth must be designed.

Silent Branding: Influence Without Exposure

Silent branding is the art of projecting influence without overexposing the individual behind it. It does not aim for anonymity but for selectivity. It lets you decide which parts of yourself or your enterprise the world sees, while keeping the core of your power, identity, and wealth insulated. Silent branding does not erase presence—it redistributes it.

In today's culture of nonstop personal branding and endless digital performance, silent branding is both rare and strategic. While most people rush to share every thought, achievement, and image, the discreet strategist does the opposite. They reveal only what strengthens their position, what reinforces their architecture, and what cannot be turned against them. Everything else stays behind the curtain.

This restraint creates a paradox. The less you reveal, the more powerful each revelation becomes. A single keynote, a carefully timed article, or a selective interview often carries more weight than a constant stream of content. Because the discreet figure does not compete for attention daily, their appearances feel deliberate—and therefore authoritative.

Silent branding also separates role from person. A founder may let the company carry the narrative while remaining invisible in day-to-day communications. A consultant may project ideas through publications, curated networks, or ghostwritten pieces, while keeping private life out of reach. Influence flows outward, but the individual stays shielded.

At its core, silent branding is about control. It means choosing when to appear, where to appear, and on what terms. It treats visibility as a tool, not as a performance.

In a world where attention is abundant but trust is scarce, this approach becomes leverage. The figure who speaks rarely, but with precision, commands more credibility than the one who floods the environment with noise. The one who appears selectively gains an aura of intention, building authority while minimizing risk.

Silent branding is not a retreat from ambition. It is ambition refined. It secures the benefits of presence—credibility, access, influence—without carrying the cost of overexposure. It is the balance between being seen and remaining sovereign.

Presence Without Personhood

One of the strongest myths in modern branding is that influence must always be tied to a face. The rise of personal branding culture has reinforced the belief that credibility cannot exist without a constant public persona. Silent branding dismantles this illusion. A brand does not need a face to create authority. It can be built on clarity, structure, and results rather than on biography.

Silent branding shifts the focus from person to system. Authority is projected through frameworks, methodologies, and outcomes, not through personality. The individual remains discreet, while the structure speaks. Presence is redistributed: the institution is the voice, not the architect behind it.

Consider a consultancy that publishes white papers, policy briefs, or insights under a strong institutional identity. These works shape debates and attract clients, yet no single author is named. Authority comes from the quality of the ideas, not the charisma of a speaker. The firm's reputation grows precisely because no single ego dominates it.

Strategic advisory groups often follow the same model. Instead of promoting partner profiles, they build authority through frameworks and case logic. The brand speaks as a system. Clients engage with methodology and outcomes, not with individuals seeking personal recognition.

Investment groups apply this principle as well. Public statements are delivered by spokespersons, external advisors, or boards—not by the principals directing strategy. Results define reputation, while decision-makers stay outside the spotlight.

This approach offers clear advantages. It attracts serious clients and partners more interested in resilience and clarity than in celebrity. It creates a brand identity that is scalable, independent of any single figure, and built for continuity. If a founder or strategist steps back, the brand remains intact because its authority was never tied to personality.

Most importantly, it preserves the separation between public and private. The world sees a coherent, professional structure. The individual's private identity stays shielded. Influence is gained, but sovereignty remains.

In Silent Branding, reputation belongs to the structure. The architect stays unseen, but the design carries authority. Power becomes independent of visibility, and credibility grows without exposure.

Strategic Voice, Not Personal Story

Branding today is saturated with storytelling. Companies dramatize their beginnings, founders are urged to display vulnerability, and executives narrate personal journeys as a way to appear relatable. This may work in consumer markets, where emotion drives sales. In high-stakes fields, it is a liability.

In finance, international law, diplomacy, private equity, or security consulting, clients are not drawn to stories of hardship or personal growth. They want clarity, stability, and assurance. A brand built on vulnerability risks signaling weakness. Silent branding recognizes this and avoids the trap. It replaces narrative with positioning–making the brand's voice about precision, not autobiography.

The question shifts from *who* is behind the brand to *what* the brand stands for. A silent brand does not ask for trust because of a founder's life story. It earns trust by defining the problems it solves, the way it approaches them, and the ground it occupies. Identity is rooted in purpose and execution, not in biography.

The consequences are significant. Growth is no longer tied to the visibility of one figure. The brand can scale through teams, processes, and systems that outlast any single personality. Authority is not dependent on charisma but on continuity.

It also creates resilience. If a founder or strategist steps aside, credibility holds. Representation can be delegated to team members, spokespersons, or intermediaries without loss of weight. The strategist continues upstream–designing frameworks, building networks, steering outcomes–while the brand speaks for itself.

Perception strengthens in the process. A silent brand does not chase attention with noise or hashtags. It signals competence by design. Its communication is sharp, its content structured, its appearances deliberate. In a landscape flooded with self-promotion, the absence of personal storytelling stands out. It becomes a mark of seriousness.

The paradox is simple. By refusing to fight for visibility, the silent brand gains authority of a different kind. It is respected not for the persona of its founder, but for the consistency of its results. Its presence is strategic, not anecdotal. Its voice is institutional, not personal. Influence comes from design, not narrative.

In the architecture of Silent Power, branding becomes leverage when it projects clarity while shielding the individual. It conveys intelligence while preserving discretion. It allows ambition to expand without turning biography into exposure.

A silent brand is not just quiet. It is intentional. It communicates less, but every word carries more weight.

Controlled Appearances and Selective Presence

Even the most discreet strategist must, at times, step into view. Absolute invisibility is neither possible nor always wise. Silent branding does not erase presence; it curates it. The task is to decide when, where, and how to appear so that visibility reinforces the structure instead of weakening it.

Controlled appearances follow the principle of selective exposure. Presence is not a constant state but a choice. A timed publication, a closed-door forum, or a signature on a document may be required, yet none of these are left to improvisation. Each is designed to project legitimacy while keeping the individual insulated from speculation or follow-up.

One way to achieve this is to publish under the name of a firm, consortium, or institution rather than as a sole author. Authority rests in the framework, not the personal biography of the contributor. The same applies to events: participation can be framed as representation of an entity instead of a showcase of individual expertise. Influence is delivered, but exposure is diluted.

When interviews are unavoidable, they are managed with strict control. Questions are filtered, personal details minimized, and responses anchored in technical clarity rather than anecdote. The objective is not silence but prevention—avoiding the drift from presence into storytelling that invites vulnerability.

Even small adjustments matter. Using initials, pseudonyms, or formal titles adds layers between the operator and the record. To an audience, the figure is present enough to command respect, yet distant enough to remain untraceable beyond the moment.

At times, visibility is treated as contingency. A funding round may require a signature, a regulatory process may demand formal disclosure, or a negotiation may call for the principal's authority. Outside those instances, the individual recedes, directing outcomes without stepping into the current.

The effect is distance. Observers see enough to confirm legitimacy but never enough to reconstruct a full profile. Timelines remain protected, legal footprints limited, reputations shielded.

Selective presence is not absence. It is deliberate curation. To appear occasionally, on one's own terms, is to remind the world of one's existence without ceding sovereignty. In Silent Power, visibility is never abolished–it is domesticated, controlled, and deployed only when it strengthens the architecture.

From Founders to Ghost Founders: Letting the Brand Speak

At its most refined, Silent Branding transforms a founder into a ghost founder–an individual who disappears from the surface of the enterprise while continuing to shape it from within. Far from diminishing influence, this withdrawal enhances it. The founder ceases to be the face of the company and instead becomes its architecture–the unseen system that directs, decides, and endures.

This invisibility is not improvised. It is engineered. Public functions–signatures, appearances, communications–are delegated to visible roles: a CEO, a managing director, or an independent board. Outwardly, the enterprise functions as if the founder were absent, yet its DNA remains defined by their frameworks, directives, and vision.

The legal design makes this possible. Holding companies, trusts, and foundations formalize control while removing it from the founder's personal identity. Professional managers or fiduciary directors appear in filings, while real authority flows through private mandates and contractual agreements. In some jurisdictions, confidentiality statutes provide further protection: a role as protector of a foundation in Liechtenstein or as beneficiary of a Jersey trust can secure influence without exposing the individual in public records.

The model extends beyond corporations. Legacy families often adopt ghost founder structures across generations, ensuring that visible leadership rotates while continuity remains intact behind the curtain. High-level consultants employ similar methods to avoid conflicts of interest, directing strategies without public exposure. Philanthropists and investors embrace it to shape institutions discreetly, preserving credibility while insulating personal identity. For political or financial figures whose reputations are under constant scrutiny, the ghost founder model balances reach with protection.

The ghost founder has not vanished. They have shifted from visibility to structure. Their name may not appear in headlines, but their system defines the brand's direction. Continuity replaces presence; sovereignty replaces recognition.

This is the essence of Silent Power: control without exposure, influence without performance, presence without personhood.

Silent Branding as Communication Without Vulnerability

Silent branding is not silence. It is not withdrawal into obscurity. It is communication stripped of vulnerability—a professional presence engineered to serve its function without undermining sovereignty.

In this framework, branding is structural. Just as power operates through systems, branding becomes one of those systems: a controlled interface between architecture and perception. To mistake the surface for the substance is to misunderstand the strategy.

The discreet strategist uses branding to regulate that interface. Recognition flows toward the structure while the individual remains protected. Presence exists, but it is detached from personal identity. Authority derives from clarity, not from constant performance.

In a culture where exposure is celebrated as strength, silent branding offers another path: credibility built on precision, authority anchored in design, and identity preserved behind structure. It is communication, but on one's own terms. It is visibility, but never captivity.

Global Navigation Strategy: Jurisdictions, Residency, and Access Without Exposure

Silent Power does not stop at structuring assets or refining branding. Its reach must extend across borders. Wealth, influence, and reputation exist in motion, moving through states, regulators, and systems. To remain sovereign, the strategist must become a global navigator.

Jurisdictions are not passive. Each has its own disclosure rules, residency triggers, tax regimes, and levels of cooperation with international frameworks. Operating across them requires choreography, not improvisation.

Residency illustrates the point. It grants access to protections and infrastructure, yet it also binds the individual to taxation and reporting. Silent operators separate physical presence from fiscal identity. Travel, business activity, and extended stays are designed to avoid automatic residency claims. Mobility is engineered to maximize access while limiting obligations.

Access is equally strategic. Banking in Switzerland, registering in Luxembourg, securing residency in the Emirates, or storing assets in

Singapore—none of these are accidents. Each is a point on a map of exposures and protections, chosen to complement the others. No authority sees the entire picture, and no regulator holds complete control.

The visible operator accepts the default rules of where they happen to live. The discreet strategist designs life across multiple systems, using law to build distance, options, and resilience.

Global navigation is not evasion. It is configuration. It uses the multiplicity of legal belonging to secure protections without inheriting unnecessary burdens.

The strategist becomes a global citizen not in lifestyle, but in structure. They belong everywhere and nowhere. They access systems of capital, networks of influence, and layers of protection without being trapped by visibility in any single jurisdiction.

This is the final layer of Silent Power: movement through global systems with presence but without exposure, with access but without surrender, with recognition but without captivity.

Residency ≠ Control, Presence ≠ Exposure

One of the most costly mistakes in global life is to confuse residency, presence, and access. They are not interchangeable. Treating them as the same leads to double taxation, regulatory captivity, and reputational risk. Silent Power begins by separating them.

Residency is legal status. It defines where the state claims the right to tax your income, demand financial disclosures, and subject you to reporting regimes. Residency is not where you sleep; it is where the law decides you belong, based on thresholds of time, economic ties, or center-of-life tests. Misunderstand this, and mobility turns into liability.

Presence is physical. It is where you spend time, hold meetings, or direct operations. It is visible but does not have to create residency if managed carefully. A strategist may spend weeks in one country and months in another while remaining non-resident in both, provided the structure avoids local tax triggers. Presence can be fluid; residency is binding.

Access is structural. It defines where you are entitled to act—where you can invest, contract, or influence—without living there or even being physically present. Access is built through legal entities, permits, and treaty rights. An investor may run a company in Singapore, hold accounts in Switzerland, and advise in Dubai without being tax resident or physically tied to any of them. Access expands reach without multiplying burdens.

The discreet strategist keeps these three layers apart. Residency is established where stability, simplicity, and privacy align. Presence is spread across countries without letting it harden into tax residence. Access is engineered through structures that open doors worldwide while leaving obligations narrowly defined.

This architecture produces freedom through separation. By refusing to let any single jurisdiction claim all three layers, the strategist avoids becoming captive. They comply everywhere but are owned nowhere. Sovereignty comes from the ability to live, move, and act across systems without being reduced to one.

The lesson is simple: where you live, where you go, and where you act must never collapse into the same answer. In Silent Power, each layer is distinct by design.

The Role of Jurisdictions in Silent Power

No single country can provide everything a strategist needs. Each has advantages, but each is limited. Silent Power does not look for the "perfect" jurisdiction; it builds a system where every jurisdiction plays a role and none holds the full picture.

Switzerland remains a cornerstone. Its legal stability, confidentiality traditions, and treaty network make it ideal for holdings, investments, and advisory platforms. Its reputation conveys legitimacy, while its privacy frameworks protect discretion.

Liechtenstein specializes in endurance. Its foundation law is among the most refined for preserving wealth across generations. It allows assets to be governed under statutory protection, shielded from political or fiscal shifts elsewhere.

The United Arab Emirates offers agility. Its tax neutrality, rapid incorporation processes, and favorable residency regimes create flexibility without excessive disclosure.

Singapore is the gateway to Asia. Its legal sophistication, fintech infrastructure, and position between East and West make it the most efficient point of entry to Asian markets. It balances credibility with speed.

Luxembourg adds European integration with structural versatility. Its fund regimes and holding vehicles are used worldwide to channel capital efficiently while keeping disclosure tightly managed.

Other jurisdictions play supporting roles. Panama and Nevis provide streamlined vehicles positioned outside many reporting frameworks. Delaware adds another layer: its strong corporate law and functional opacity at the LLC level make it useful for hybrid or domestic structures where visibility must be managed carefully.

The strategist's art lies in orchestration. A company may be incorporated in Luxembourg, its accounts in Switzerland, its management in the UAE, assets stored in Singapore, while the principal resides elsewhere. Each part works. None reveals the whole.

This is jurisdictional diversification—the legal form of compartmentalized power. By distributing roles, resilience is built. No regulator, journalist, or adversary can reconstruct the system from a single angle.

At its highest level, Silent Power is not refuge in one country. It is mastery across many.

Mobility as a Strategic Asset

Mobility, once treated as a lifestyle perk or a matter of convenience, has become one of the sharpest instruments in the strategist's arsenal. In a world governed by interconnected tax regimes, compliance frameworks, and surveillance systems, where you spend your time is no longer just personal preference—it is a structural choice with legal and financial weight. Managed intentionally, mobility stops being movement and becomes protection.

Strategic mobility shields individuals from permanent establishment risks, helps them sidestep common residency triggers, and allows them to work jurisdictional thresholds—such as the often-misunderstood 183-day rule—without falling into unnecessary obligations. It reduces exposure in high-surveillance or litigious environments, ensuring that physical presence does not automatically translate into vulnerability.

Silent operators treat mobility as a built-in layer of design, not as an afterthought. Some secure second residencies or additional citizenships through legal investment programs. These give them banking rights, corporate privileges, and visa-free travel while stopping short of binding them to fiscal residence. Others use favorable regimes such as non-domicile systems, which exempt certain foreign income when residence is structured correctly.

At the highest level, mobility becomes cyclical. Primary residence is shifted periodically—not to evade responsibility, but to balance visibility and obligations across borders. The point is to make sure no single jurisdiction holds all three levers at once: residency, presence, and control.

In a handful of proactive countries, strategists even negotiate their tax status before arrival. Through advance rulings or binding agreements, they define their fiscal terms from the outset, turning relocation into a contract rather than a gamble.

Mobility, paired with disciplined legal design, ceases to be a lifestyle preference. It becomes jurisdictional self-determination. It gives individuals the power to decide not only where they live, but under what rules. It ensures that presence is chosen, not imposed, and that access to the global system does not collapse into global exposure.

In the architecture of Silent Power, mobility is not escape. It is configuration. It turns borders from obstacles into instruments of sovereignty.

Legal Presence Without Personal Risk

Global reach no longer requires physical presence. With careful structuring, it is possible to direct companies, control assets, and influence markets without leaving a personal trace in the jurisdictions where they operate. This is not avoidance—it is deliberate design. Silent Power uses the law itself to separate ownership, management, and benefit so that influence crosses borders while liability stays contained.

The mechanics are straightforward. A principal may guide a company's direction without being listed as a director by working through fiduciaries. They may hold real estate through a fund or corporate vehicle managed elsewhere, keeping their name out of land registries. They may control accounts where fiduciary directors or appointed officers sign officially, while real instructions flow through private mandates. Authority is not diminished by absence—it is exercised through contracts, capital, and design.

Other channels reinforce this approach. Capital injections, licenses secured through affiliates, or layered ownership arrangements allow substantial influence without ever appearing in registries. Local systems see compliance; the global strategist keeps control.

Certain jurisdictions actively facilitate this kind of remote architecture. The United Arab Emirates allows companies, bank accounts, and residency permits without extended physical presence. Luxembourg offers fund vehicles that can be governed with minimal local board involvement. Switzerland permits the remote management of holding entities if governance standards and reporting are observed. Each of these examples blends compliance with discretion.

The effectiveness of such systems rests on three pillars. First, airtight documentation: every mandate and fiduciary relationship must be legally binding and properly recorded. Second, substance: structures must be coherent and functional, not hollow shells. Third, separation of roles: those who appear in filings or act as signatories are distinct from those who actually shape strategy, ensuring distance between what is visible and what is decisive.

When these elements align, presence becomes optional. A strategist can remain absent from registries while exercising complete command. They may never set foot in the jurisdiction, yet their influence guides its companies, shapes its investments, and directs its flows of capital.

This is legal presence without personal risk: acting globally without being captured locally, gaining access without assuming exposure, and projecting influence without leaving the kind of footprints that compromise sovereignty.

Sovereign Logic: Living by Design, Not by Default

Global strategy is often mistaken for tax planning, second residencies, or shifting assets from one country to another. Those are details. The real subject is sovereignty. It is the discipline of shaping your legal and financial identity, your obligations, and your public footprint according to design—not according to the defaults of a single state. To live sovereignly is to take authorship of your own position in the world.

Silent Power is the method that makes this authorship possible. It lets you draw clear lines: presence without exposure, residency without captivity, access without vulnerability. It gives you the freedom to decide where you live because the system fits your long-term goals, not because geography or habit forces the choice. It allows you to engage in multiple jurisdictions without being trapped by any of them.

This approach is not about running from responsibility. It is about refusing to drift into obligations by accident—refusing to let birthplace or convenience dictate your fate. Systems can be negotiated. Jurisdictions can complement one another. And the map of your commitments can be redrawn if you take the time to design it.

The strategist who follows this path is not a wanderer without roots. Their roots are real, but they lie in structure rather than in soil. Their continuity does not come from a passport alone but from the architecture that protects their assets, shields their reputation, and preserves their independence.

Sovereign logic also changes the meaning of belonging. You are not defined by where you were born, or by where you happen to sleep, or by what a registry declares. You belong where your system works, where your architecture is functional, and where your interests align. And you belong nowhere that holds you against your will.

This is the essence of Silent Power at the global scale: living by design instead of by default. Borders become tools. Jurisdictions become parts of a system. Presence becomes a choice, not a constraint. It is not invisibility—it is authorship. It is the ability to function in the world as a sovereign actor, visible only when useful, and silent enough to remain free.

Final Note - Strategic Discretion Requires Personal Architecture

Residency is not one thing. To a tax office it means one set of rules, to immigration another, to healthcare systems another still, and to banks yet another for compliance. A single person can be tax resident in one country, registered for benefits in a second, and culturally tied to a third. Each claim is different, and each carries its own consequences.

If you want discretion, you must separate these layers. Confusing fiscal residency with immigration status, or banking access with cultural belonging, is a mistake that creates unnecessary exposure. The strategist maps each claim on its own terms, making sure no single jurisdiction controls the whole picture.

But law is only half the equation. The other half is self-knowledge. There is no universal template for discretion. There is only personal architecture. Every individual brings a different mix of passports, resources, risks, ambitions, and constraints. The structure has to fit that mix.

Your legal background and citizenships define the starting line: which states already hold claims, which treaties apply, and what protections or obligations you carry automatically. Your economic position shapes the tools at your disposal—trusts, foundations, holding companies, or partnerships. Risk tolerance and political exposure set the boundary between aggressive structuring and defensive preservation.

Family and succession needs add another layer: whether the design must protect continuity, enable distribution, or prevent conflict across generations. Lifestyle choices—climate, culture, rhythm, security—decide where presence is not just possible but sustainable. Above all, long-term goals give the direction: whether the aim is creation of wealth, preservation, mobility, personal freedom, or legacy.

Some build for permanence, creating dynastic systems meant to last for decades. Others build for agility, reducing complexity and maximizing flexibility. Some place tax neutrality above all. Others simply want stability or a safer environment for their families.

Silent Power does not prescribe a formula. It opens a framework in which deliberate choices can be made—quietly, without noise, and in alignment with intent.

Every decision—about residency, ownership, structure, or mobility—must reflect the strategist's own values and tempo. Discretion is not a single path. It is the freedom to draw your own, deliberately and with full authorship.

CHAPTER III - STRUCTURING CONTROL WITHOUT EXPOSURE

Control Without Ownership

The architecture of Silent Power is never defined by what is visible. It rests in the forces that shape outcomes even when they remain absent from the surface. In an age where ownership has become shorthand for exposure—through registries, compliance rules, and automated reporting—the strongest position is almost never the one formally recognized. Real strength lies in guiding decisions from outside the spotlight.

To build control without exposure is to accept a paradox: the louder your title, the weaker your position. The strategist learns early that ownership and control must be split, and that attribution should never fall on the same head that carries influence. The system is designed so the individual directs, benefits, and governs, yet never appears in the public or legal frame.

This is not some obscure trick. It is mainstream practice in corporate law, fiduciary administration, estate planning, and international investment. Family offices rely on it to protect dynastic wealth while remaining discreet. Cross-border investors use it to survive conflicting disclosure rules. Anyone who has seen how a single public entry in one registry can cascade into exposures elsewhere understands why this discipline is indispensable.

Structuring authority in this way does not mean ignoring compliance. It means exercising authority indirectly—through contracts, mandates, and fiduciary roles that meet the law while keeping the principal insulated. Properly done, the structure is resilient. Even if one layer is challenged, the real center of control sits safely behind it.

Principles of Control Without Ownership

The foundation of this discipline is a simple but overlooked rule: ownership is not the same as control. Ownership is the name on the deed, the shareholder recorded in the registry, the beneficiary in an official declaration. Control is something different—it is the power to direct, to allocate, to decide. The two may overlap, but they do not need to.

The strategist embraces this separation. The objective is to keep decision-making and benefit while stripping away the visibility that legal title creates. Control flows through instruments rather than through appearances. It can be secured with a power of attorney, embedded in governance rules that detach voting rights from economic rights, or written into internal contracts that never touch the public record.

This is not marginal law—it is the fabric of modern systems. Corporations are run by boards whose members may own nothing. Trusts and foundations are steered by protectors or trustees who hold no title yet decide the fate of assets. Investment funds are managed by companies acting on behalf of silent investors. In every case, ownership sits in one place, while control lives elsewhere.

In high-stakes, cross-border contexts, this separation is not optional. A name on a shareholder list can attract litigation, taxes, or reputational fire. A signature in a registry may invite scrutiny far beyond the original jurisdiction. Control without ownership works the other way: authority is exercised, but the traces left behind are minimal. This is not concealment. It is configuration. It is the deliberate placement of visibility where it carries the least risk, and influence where it carries the most weight.

Control as Function, Not Status

Modern law itself distinguishes between legal ownership, beneficial ownership, and effective control. At first glance these may appear interchangeable, but they describe different realities. Legal ownership is the title on the books. Beneficial ownership is the right to receive value. Effective control is the ability to steer outcomes regardless of what the documents say.

These three categories need not align. In fact, in strategic structuring they are often pulled apart on purpose. By detaching title, benefit, and control, the strategist ensures that power is real but exposure is limited.

Take a family office as an example. A trust may hold the voting rights of a company, keeping direction in the hands of trustees or protectors. Profits flow to heirs through a distribution mechanism, but the heirs themselves are absent from governance. Legal title sits in one place, economic benefit in another, strategic control in a third. No single participant holds the full picture.

Or consider a founder who resigns from the board, installing professional directors in the visible roles. On paper, their involvement is over. In practice, private shareholder agreements and irrevocable mandates guarantee they still shape every strategic decision. To the public, it looks like withdrawal. In reality, it is architecture: exposure is reduced while influence remains intact.

Investors use the same principle in private markets. An individual may never appear in a fund's registry, yet through discretionary mandates they direct how capital is deployed. The market sees only the manager. The real instructions come from elsewhere.

The point is consistent: control is not a badge you wear; it is a function you embed. It resides in the mechanics of decision-making, not in the name that shows up in filings. To those reading registries, the authority seems absent. To those who designed the system, the authority is exactly where they placed it—beyond reach, shielded by structure.

Separation of Functions for Legal Protection

In the design of Silent Power, discretion is never achieved by concentrating roles in one pair of hands. It is achieved by distributing them. To keep control discreet, the strategist separates the essential functions that define how any asset or entity is managed. Ownership, benefit, control, and administration may look simple on paper, but when allocated across different legal actors they form the backbone of resilience.

The title holder is the name that shows up in official registries, deeds, or filings. The beneficiary is the person entitled to enjoy value—dividends, income, or direct use of an asset. The controller is the strategist who defines direction and sets policy. And the administrator is the professional who ensures that reports are filed, accounts are reconciled, and compliance is maintained.

If all these functions converge in one person, exposure becomes immediate. That individual stands as owner, decision-maker, beneficiary, and administrator, with no separation between personal identity and structural function. A legal claim, a regulatory inquiry, or a reputational hit cuts straight to the center.

When the roles are split, the opposite occurs. The title may sit with a company or fiduciary; benefits may flow to heirs or family; control may be secured by mandates or contracts; administration can be handled by professionals. Each part is genuine, but no single one reveals the whole picture. Together, they deliver insulation against claims, flexibility across jurisdictions, strategic distance from reputational risk, and the ability to adapt as rules evolve.

This logic is not abstract. It sits at the heart of trust law, where settlor, trustee, and beneficiary are always distinct. It underpins corporate governance, where shareholders and directors play different roles, and boards make decisions even when beneficial owners remain silent. It shapes philanthropy, where donors step back and foundations are managed by professional boards, with the donor's intent preserved in statutes or letters of wishes.

The purpose is not to avoid accountability but to prevent any single person from becoming the weak link through which an entire system can be compromised. Separation distributes exposure, reduces vulnerability, and preserves continuity even under pressure. In strategic architecture, separation is not fragility—it is strength.

Control Through Architecture, Not Authority

In common imagination, control means visible authority: the one at the head of the table, signing documents, giving orders in public. Silent Power turns this idea on its head. Control does not come from occupying the visible seat. It comes from designing the table, defining the seats, and writing the rules by which decisions are made.

Authority exercised through visibility is fragile. Control exercised through architecture endures. Voting rights, for example, need not be wielded in person. They can be embedded in shareholder agreements, irrevocable mandates, or governance protocols that assign power to proxies acting for the strategist. Decision-making authority does not need a podium. It can be built quietly into corporate statutes or management rules that define how choices are made long before a meeting begins.

This approach lets the strategist remain absent yet omnipresent. Veto powers may be buried in clauses invisible to the public. Appointment rights may be tied to a special class of shares. Removal mechanisms may exist in contracts seen only by insiders. Even the flow of benefits can be routed through entities or accounts that never require the principal's direct signature.

In this model, the strategist is no longer a visible leader but an invisible architect. Their influence is not performed; it is embedded. They may never appear in registries, reports, or organizational charts, yet their intent shapes every outcome because the structure itself is designed to reflect it.

This is discretion in practice. Authority can be challenged, contested, or replaced. Architecture cannot. Once in place, it governs quietly without the need to defend itself in public.

Nominee Structures and Fiduciary Roles

Across the world's legal systems, it is both lawful and routine to appoint third parties to occupy visible positions on behalf of those who prefer to remain discreet. This is the basis of nominee structures and fiduciary roles: mechanisms that separate surface responsibility from underlying control while staying within the law.

Registers, deeds, and contracts demand names. But the individual who appears on paper does not have to be the one in charge. Nominees and fiduciaries allow the strategist to keep trusted figures on the surface while decisions continue to flow from private agreements, mandates, and contracts behind the scenes.

These arrangements are not exotic. They are everyday practice in banking, commerce, and wealth management. Private banks rely on fiduciary officers to shield clients from direct visibility. Real estate deals in countries with public land registries often involve nominee directors or shareholders to avoid tying property to personal names. International trade contracts are signed by professional intermediaries who absorb the reputational or political risks. Family offices build entire fiduciary boards to manage wealth across borders while keeping principals off the record.

When designed correctly, nominee structures deliver a balance otherwise impossible: the entity remains fully operational and compliant, while the principal stays protected. Fiduciaries carry the visible responsibility, but their scope is tightly defined by private agreements that ensure the strategist's intent prevails.

The true strength lies in layering. One nominee may hold a directorship, another entity may own shares, and a trustee may hold voting rights. Each layer creates distance. Even if one point is scrutinized, the full system is never exposed. This is not concealment but configuration: every role is real and documented, yet no single node reveals the core.

Importantly, nominee and fiduciary structures are not loopholes. They are regulated, recognized, and widely accepted. What distinguishes their role in Silent Power is intent. For the strategist, they are not mere conveniences—they are shields of sovereignty. The visible figure carries the surface role. The fiduciary manages compliance. The strategist remains behind the design: unseen, but in command.

Definition of a Nominee and Fiduciary Role

At the core of many discreet structures stand two complementary figures: the nominee and the fiduciary. They are often confused, but their roles are distinct. Both exist to create distance between the strategist and the surface of the system, without weakening either control or compliance.

A nominee is the visible actor. Their name appears in official records–company registries, shareholder lists, or corporate deeds–instead of the principal's. They do not act independently. Their decisions are guided, often in detail, by private instructions. The nominee occupies the public seat, while the strategist remains behind the design.

A fiduciary plays a different part. They are not placeholders but holders of responsibility. Trustees, directors, protectors, and proxy holders all fall under this category. Fiduciaries are bound by legal duties to act in the best interest of the party they represent. Those duties are enforceable; they are not symbolic. A fiduciary who breaches them faces liability, which is why these roles are carefully defined and regulated.

Neither nominees nor fiduciaries operate in a legal vacuum. Many jurisdictions require them to be licensed, registered, or subject to professional oversight. Their authority, scope, and limits are usually spelled out in private agreements–mandates, service contracts, or declarations of trust. These agreements make sure their actions reflect the principal's intent while protecting the strategist from unnecessary exposure.

The powers attached to these roles are flexible. They may be limited, revocable, or subject to conditions depending on the jurisdiction.

In some cases, the arrangement is entirely private and invisible unless disclosure is compelled by law. In others, transparency rules require partial or full disclosure, yet the principal still benefits from contractual distance.

In practice, nominees and fiduciaries act as filters. They absorb visibility, carry administrative responsibility, and often shield the strategist from reputational risk. The public sees the nominee, regulators deal with the fiduciary, but influence flows from elsewhere.

This is not about avoidance—it is alignment. The structure stays compliant, the asset remains operational, and the strategist preserves sovereignty.

Lawful Uses of Nominee Arrangements

Nominee structures are not loopholes. They are part of mainstream corporate and fiduciary practice, recognized and regulated in advanced legal systems. Used correctly, they allow individuals to retain control while minimizing personal visibility—a critical balance in jurisdictions where exposure can quickly become vulnerability.

The logic is straightforward: public systems demand names, but the name provided does not have to be the one exercising influence. The nominee appears in the public role, while contracts and mandates ensure that benefits and decisions remain with the principal.

In corporate life, this may mean a director sits abroad on behalf of the company while the investor stays off public registries. Shares may be registered to a service provider or fiduciary, with parallel agreements confirming who truly holds economic rights. The public record tells one story; the private instruments tell the real one.

Banking provides another example. Accounts may be opened under a corporate entity, with a fiduciary officer signing on behalf of the principal. The bank deals with the officer, but access to funds remains tied to the instructions of the strategist. Compliance is satisfied, while discretion is preserved.

Real estate can be managed the same way. Property may be deeded in the name of a trust or foundation. The principal enjoys use or income under private agreements while remaining absent from registries. To the outside world, the property belongs to the entity. In practice, it is governed by the strategist's design.

Such structures are particularly valuable for people in sensitive positions: politicians, judges, investigative journalists, or senior officials who must avoid conflicts of interest and protect personal security. Nominee arrangements allow them to remain compliant while separating professional accountability from private stewardship.

Examples are widespread. Switzerland permits fiduciary directors and administrative vehicles that separate presence from ownership. Luxembourg provides specialized holding and family wealth structures. The UAE authorizes nominee setups in its free zones. Liechtenstein foundations, protected by confidentiality statutes, safeguard wealth across generations. Similar mechanisms exist in Malta, Singapore, and Hong Kong.

Far from undermining compliance, nominee arrangements often strengthen it. They provide functional anonymity: visibility where it is legally required, silence where it is not. This gives the strategist the ability to operate securely, manage assets effectively, and preserve sovereignty across borders.

Elements of a Secure and Effective Nominee Agreement

A nominee or fiduciary arrangement is only as strong as the agreement that supports it. Without precise documentation and careful jurisdictional choices, what should be a shield can turn into a vulnerability. For the discreet strategist, the agreement is not a formality but the blueprint that defines whether control holds or collapses.

At its core lies a written contract. It may take the form of a mandate, fiduciary letter, or nominee declaration, but the purpose is always the same: to codify the relationship, to separate visibility from control, and to ensure that every action reflects the principal's intent.

Several provisions are critical. First, the agreement must set strict limits on liability, preventing the nominee from creating obligations beyond what has been authorized. Second, it must define with clarity the scope of authority: signing documents, attending meetings, opening accounts. Anything left vague is an invitation to risk.

Instructions and reporting are another pillar. The contract must explain how directives are delivered—whether in writing, electronically, or through notarized acts—and whether the nominee must provide feedback. Some structures favor silence, activating only upon instruction. Others impose regular reporting to balance discretion with accountability.

Exit conditions are essential. The framework must anticipate disputes, incapacity, death, or outside legal pressure. It should state how a nominee can be replaced, how mandates can be revoked, and under what conditions the arrangement terminates. Without these clauses, a temporary safeguard can become a liability.

Jurisdiction matters as much as content. Agreements governed by Swiss or Liechtenstein law benefit from strong traditions of fiduciary practice and statutory confidentiality. English law offers predictability and enforceability in arbitration. Choosing the wrong jurisdiction can undo years of careful planning.

Often, two layers of documents are used. Public filings show the nominee's role. Private agreements, sometimes notarized or sealed, preserve the principal's authority. The public layer satisfies regulators. The private layer safeguards sovereignty.

When drafted with precision, the nominee agreement becomes more than protection. It becomes a tool of design: a way to exercise control without exposure, to operate fully within the law while preserving discretion. In the architecture of Silent Power, it is not a defensive shield but an active instrument of sovereignty.

Ethical and Compliance Considerations

Nominee and fiduciary frameworks occupy a clear and legitimate place in the legal and financial order. They are recognized in statutes, subject to regulation, and used daily by investors, families, and institutions worldwide. Their strength—separating visibility from control—is also the reason regulators examine them closely. The strategist must therefore understand: Silent Power is not about ignoring compliance, but about designing discretion that can stand up to scrutiny.

A compliant structure begins with respect for substance and for disclosure duties where they apply. If a jurisdiction requires proof of management, financial reporting, or the submission of beneficial ownership data to regulators, these conditions must be met. Discretion does not mean concealment. It means showing exactly what is required, and nothing more.

Every arrangement must also be defensible under audit. Whether examined by a tax authority, a bank, or a court, the system must make sense. Contracts must be valid, the logic coherent, the design consistent. A fragile setup that collapses under basic questioning is not discretion; it is recklessness. True resilience comes from frameworks that survive inspection.

KYC and AML procedures form another layer of strength. Fiduciaries, nominees, and service providers must all perform these checks. They protect not only regulators, but also the strategist, who benefits from the legitimacy such processes confer. Discretion is not achieved by avoiding scrutiny but by channeling it in ways that are predictable and controlled.

Most importantly, these structures must never serve as vehicles for fraud, tax evasion, or unlawful concealment. Discretion is lawful. Deception is not. Silent Power rests on authorship—on designing systems that protect sovereignty without crossing the line into illegality.

In practice, this means clarity behind the curtain even if public records remain minimal. Mandates, agreements, and delegations must be properly drafted, enforceable, and aligned with law. The strategist may remain unseen, but their architecture must remain solid. Only then does discretion function as a shield rather than a liability.

Foundations, Trusts, and Hybrid Entities

Nominees and fiduciaries provide distance in the short and medium term. For those who want permanence—for those intent on preserving and governing wealth across generations—more advanced instruments are required: foundations, trusts, and hybrids. These vehicles introduce autonomy. They are not placeholders for an individual but full legal systems in themselves, with the power to hold, govern, and transmit assets beyond the lifespan of their creator.

Their autonomy is their strength. A foundation or trust is designed to govern itself through statutes, trust deeds, or internal rules that survive political upheaval, family disputes, or even the absence of the founder. Properly built, such structures endure without constant intervention.

Contrary to common belief, these tools are not reserved for billionaires or dynastic families. Entrepreneurs who move across borders, consultants balancing exposure and protection, expatriates navigating multiple systems, and investors seeking resilience all use them. Their value lies in neutrality: they position wealth beyond the reach of any one state while remaining fully compliant within all.

A foundation, common in Liechtenstein, Panama, or Switzerland, has no shareholders. It is directed by a council or board according to statutes, letters of wishes, or reserved powers. Its assets are legally detached from personal ownership and directed by governance rules designed by the founder.

Trusts, rooted in Anglo-Saxon law, create separation by assigning legal ownership to trustees while economic benefit flows to beneficiaries. They are highly adaptable: the trust deed can embed vetoes, protections, or evolving beneficiary lists. Their strength lies in invisibility—trusts are legal relationships, not entities, often requiring no public registration.

Hybrid entities combine features. Private interest foundations may hold corporate powers. Partnerships may incorporate trust-like mechanisms for allocating benefits. These hybrids allow structures to adapt to mixed civil- and common-law environments or to the demands of cross-border families and businesses.

Used properly, these vehicles do more than preserve wealth. They embed discretion into the system itself. The strategist may vanish from records, but the structure persists—silent, compliant, and sovereign.

Private Foundations: Ownership Without Owners

One of the most refined instruments of Silent Power is the private foundation. It exists as a legal person in its own right, created not to belong to anyone but to serve a purpose. Unlike companies or partnerships, it has no owners. Its assets are dedicated irrevocably to the objectives defined by its statutes. From that moment, the foundation lives independently.

That autonomy makes it uniquely powerful. Foundations can hold assets indefinitely—company shares, real estate, intellectual property, art, or financial portfolios—without being linked to the vulnerabilities of personal title. The foundation itself becomes the owner of record, while governance rules allow the founder's intent to guide decisions.

Beneficiaries receive benefits according to internal documents, not as owners. Lists may remain unpublished, known only to the board or a protector, and can evolve over time. This provides flexibility and privacy in how wealth is distributed.

Control is exercised through governance. Boards, councils, or protectors oversee decisions, but their authority is set out in the founding deed. Veto rights, appointment powers, or oversight mechanisms allow the founder's will to endure well beyond their lifetime. Authority thus becomes structural rather than personal.

Jurisdiction matters. Liechtenstein offers advanced regimes for generational wealth. Switzerland provides robust frameworks for public-interest foundations. Panama, Curaçao, Austria, and Malta offer alternatives tailored to private wealth. Each balances privacy and regulation differently, and the strategist chooses accordingly.

When designed with precision, a foundation becomes an invisible container of power. It owns, governs, and distributes without exposing the architect. It is not a mask but a vessel, one of the purest forms of control without visibility.

Trusts: The Anglo-Saxon Standard of Invisible Control

If foundations are the civil-law archetype, trusts are the Anglo-Saxon standard. A trust is not a legal entity but a legal relationship. A settlor transfers assets to a trustee, who manages them for beneficiaries. It has no shareholders, no registry, and no independent personality. It exists in law but remains largely invisible—an arrangement of duties rather than a body corporate.

This invisibility is its strength. In most jurisdictions, trusts require no public filing of deeds, no disclosure of beneficiaries, no registration in public databases. They are enforceable under law, yet shielded from unnecessary exposure.

The trust deed provides immense flexibility. It defines how assets are managed, what powers trustees have, and how benefits are distributed. Assets in trust are no longer legally owned by the settlor, insulating them from certain claims, taxation, or visibility. Beneficiaries may be confidential, undefined at the outset, or conditional. The structure can evolve as circumstances change.

For the strategist, the trust offers a way to control wealth without being visible as its owner. Authority is exercised through the deed and the duties it imposes, not through a name in a registry. Like the foundation, it ensures that discretion and sovereignty are written into the architecture itself.

Trusts: Forms and Strategic Use

Trusts are recognized throughout the common law world—from the United Kingdom and the United States to Canada, Singapore, Hong Kong, and the Caribbean financial hubs. Their adaptability has given rise to multiple specialized forms.

Discretionary trusts leave distributions to the trustee's judgment. Beneficiaries have no automatic claim, which preserves both flexibility and protection. Purpose trusts, by contrast, exist to pursue a defined objective rather than to serve named individuals; they are widely used for philanthropic missions, for holding voting rights, or for securing long-term governance. Protector or enforcer models add another layer: a third party is empowered to oversee the trustee, ensuring fidelity to the settlor's intent while maintaining separation between influence and visibility.

When combined with holding companies, layered mandates, and hybrid governance, trusts function as invisible engines of control.

They allow assets to move across borders, preserve intent across generations, bypass probate courts, and withstand disputes—all while remaining outside the glare of public records.

A well-drafted trust is not a loophole. It is one of the oldest and most tested legal instruments in history, relied upon by families, investors, and institutions for centuries. What makes it indispensable in Silent Power is its capacity to transform control into architecture: authority embedded in a private legal relationship, enforceable under law yet shielded from visibility.

The trust demonstrates the central principle of discretion: ownership is not required to govern, and visibility is not required for authority. In the strategist's hands, it becomes more than a container of wealth. It is a living framework of invisible control.

Hybrid Entities: Mixing Corporate and Fiduciary Logic

Traditional tools—companies, trusts, and foundations—each have strengths and limits. Companies are efficient for operations but tie ownership directly to visibility. Trusts and foundations excel at separating ownership, benefit, and control, yet may lack the flexibility needed for commercial ventures. To bridge these gaps, a number of jurisdictions have developed hybrid vehicles—structures that combine corporate stability with fiduciary depth, offering unmatched configurability for those operating across borders.

These hybrids embody the logic of Silent Power. They allow influence to be exercised through architecture rather than title, blending the invisibility of fiduciary arrangements with the recognition and continuity of corporate forms.

Liechtenstein and Austria have refined the Stiftung, a foundation-like entity that can own companies, manage funds, or act as a holding platform for multigenerational wealth. It has no shareholders but retains commercial capacity, merging foundation principles with corporate functions.

Private Trust Companies (PTCs), common in Cayman or Jersey, are another model. A PTC is created to act as trustee for one or more family trusts. It lets a family retain indirect control over governance while benefiting from the fiduciary shield and operational framework of a corporate body. Decision-making remains familiar, yet the structure operates under regulated fiduciary standards.

In the United Kingdom, Family Investment Companies (FICs) have gained traction as substitutes for trusts. They separate control from benefit through tailored shareholder agreements, often granting parents voting rights while children hold economic interests. The result is a corporate shell functioning with the long-term planning logic of a fiduciary system.

Special Purpose Vehicles (SPVs) and dedicated holding companies serve similar roles worldwide. They isolate projects, contain liabilities, or achieve tax neutrality. By aligning jurisdiction and purpose, they act as modular building blocks for sophisticated global structures.

The strength of these hybrids lies in their blend of flexibility, discretion, and continuity. They allow wealth to pass across generations without triggering full succession at each stage. They adapt to both civil and common law systems, serving families and investors whose assets and heirs are spread across multiple traditions.

For entrepreneurs, cross-border investors, or philanthropists balancing private intent with public obligations, hybrid entities have become cornerstones of modern sovereignty. They prove that control need not equal exposure—and that by merging the best of corporate and fiduciary traditions, one can design structures that are both invisible and enduring.

Control Through Design, Not Possession

What unites these advanced vehicles—trusts, foundations, holding companies, hybrids—is their ability to separate what most assume must coincide: ownership, control, and benefit. They convert power from something fragile and personal into something structural and resilient. In such frameworks, the strategist is present in every decision yet absent from every registry. Power is not diluted by invisibility; it is refined into architecture.

The true architect does not need to appear as the executor. They define the rules, but others carry them out. Their presence is embedded not in signatures or filings, but in private instruments: veto rights written into statutes, appointment powers secured in shareholder agreements, instructions hidden in deeds or letters of wishes. These clauses—enforceable under law yet shielded from public view—ensure the strategist's hand shapes every outcome, even if their name never surfaces.

Execution belongs to others. Fiduciaries, boards, and advisors occupy the visible seats, sign contracts, and satisfy regulators. But they do not define intent. They are stewards of a design written upstream.

This approach achieves what direct ownership never can: continuity. A person who owns everything outright becomes a single point of failure. Death, litigation, political pressure, or reputational attack can unravel their influence in an instant. But when authority is embedded in architecture, the strategist ceases to be the system's weak point. The structure itself ensures survival.

This is the essence of control without possession: authority that endures beyond visibility, systems that outlast presence, and continuity that extends beyond one lifetime. It is not disappearance but precision—the ability to shape outcomes without exposure, to govern without noise, and to preserve influence without tying it to a name.

In Silent Power, possession is fragile. Design is enduring.

Power of Attorney and Delegated Signatures

Influence does not always require a visible title or a public seat at the table. Some of the most effective strategies for operating discreetly are rooted in something far simpler: the quiet force of signature. Authority does not need to be paraded. It can be exercised invisibly, through the ability to direct, approve, or block actions with legally delegated powers.

This is where powers of attorney (PoA) and delegated signature rights become essential. Recognized in nearly every legal system, they allow a principal to grant another person or entity the authority to act on their behalf—without requiring the principal's name to appear in registries or formal positions. The scope can be as narrow as authorizing a single contract or as broad as conferring full management powers over a company, a portfolio, or an estate.

The strength of these instruments lies in their adaptability. A PoA can be broad or narrow, revocable or irrevocable, temporary or enduring. It can authorize the attorney-in-fact to move funds, negotiate with regulators, transfer property, or vote in shareholder meetings. To the outside world, the signatory appears to hold authority. In truth, they are carrying out a private mandate, every act tied back to the strategist.

This approach secures two objectives. It allows the strategist to remain absent from the surface—their name never appears as shareholder or director—while their decisions are executed with full legal force. It also ensures continuity. Transactions proceed across borders even when the strategist is not present or listed in any public role.

In practice, delegated signatures are everywhere. A family office may empower a fiduciary director to execute contracts within strict limits. An investor may instruct a trustee to approve transactions on their behalf, with conditions spelled out in a mandate. In sensitive negotiations, a representative may be authorized to sign agreements or veto decisions, while the architect of the system remains in the background.

Properly designed, these mandates are not loopholes. They are legal extensions of sovereignty. They embody the principle that power resides not in appearances but in the ability to decide when, how, and through whom authority flows.

In the architecture of Silent Power, the signature does more than confirm decisions—it conceals them. Authority is embedded in design, not in display. And delegated signatures remain one of the quietest, most decisive instruments of invisible control.

The Power of Attorney as a Tool of Silent Operation

At first glance, a power of attorney looks unremarkable: a document through which a principal authorizes an agent to act in their place. Yet within Silent Power, this modest instrument carries extraordinary weight. Drafted with precision, it becomes a surgical tool of invisible influence.

The PoA's versatility is its strength. It may cover a single action—signing a contract, transferring property, casting a vote—or grant wide authority over financial and legal matters. It may be designed to expire after a short term or endure regardless of circumstance. It may be revocable at will or structured to remain binding until a specific condition is met. Each configuration serves a strategic purpose.

Its real power lies in separating function from appearance. A strategist may not appear in registries, board minutes, or shareholder lists, yet through a PoA they can:

- Authorize transactions and contracts
- Open, manage, or close accounts
- Direct corporate restructuring or transfers
- Vote in assemblies or exercise veto rights
- Negotiate with regulators or counterparties

The authority is binding in law but invisible in public records. In jurisdictions where PoAs are not publicly registered, the effect is even stronger: the mandate remains entirely private, enforceable in court but unseen by outsiders.

For the discreet strategist, the PoA is not about convenience. It is a channel through which control flows quietly, decisions are made without attribution, and sovereignty is preserved without display. It proves that true power often speaks in silence—through contracts that govern outcomes while leaving the architect unseen.

Delegated Signature vs. Formal Position

Conventional thinking equates authority with office: directors sit on boards, shareholders appear in registries, officers hold visible titles. Silent Power dismantles this assumption. Influence is not determined by who occupies the seat but by who controls the signature.

Delegated signature rights can be granted internally, beyond the view of outsiders. A board may empower a trusted executive to sign on its behalf. A settlor may authorize a protector to act under a private mandate. A holding company may permit a manager to sign for its subsidiary, while the strategist remains absent from filings. In each case, the authority to act is real, but the responsibility to appear falls elsewhere.

This distinction is critical. Capacity to decide can be separated from visibility. A strategist may never appear in official documents, yet every action depends on their private approval. On paper, they are absent. In practice, nothing moves without their consent.

Layered signatures strengthen this further. A transaction may require two approvals: one from a visible director, another from a mandate-holder acting under private authority. The public sees compliance. The strategist ensures nothing happens without their unseen hand.

Delegated signatures capture the essence of Silent Power: influence without exposure. Authority exists, but it lives in mandates and architecture rather than in public seats. The strategist governs not by being visible at the head of the table, but by ensuring the table cannot function without their unseen signature.

Limits, Risks, and Legal Validity

No instrument of silent operation is without limits, and the power of attorney is no exception. While it offers exceptional flexibility and discretion, its strength depends entirely on how carefully it is drafted and how rigorously it is applied. Overreliance on delegated authority without proper documentation or oversight can invite suspicion, especially in sensitive jurisdictions or when large transactions are involved. A tool designed as a shield can quickly be reinterpreted as abuse if the framework lacks coherence or safeguards.

For a PoA to be enforceable, it must meet formal requirements. It should always be in writing, and in many jurisdictions notarization is necessary to confirm authenticity. If the document is to be used abroad, apostille or legalization procedures are often required to secure recognition across borders. Its scope must be precise—defining what the agent may do, under what circumstances, and for how long. Vague mandates are vulnerable mandates. Without clarity, the risk of challenge or misuse grows dramatically.

A well-drafted PoA also anticipates its own termination. In most systems, powers of attorney are presumed revocable at the will of the principal, unless clearly stated otherwise. Even irrevocable mandates generally include specific exit conditions to protect against abuse or unforeseen conflict. Experienced drafters build in these safeguards, ensuring that authority lasts only as long as it aligns with the principal's intent.

Another limitation lies in the very nature of the instrument. In many jurisdictions, a PoA ceases to be valid upon the incapacity or death of the principal. This makes it unsuitable as a stand-alone tool for long-term planning. A PoA can provide control in the short or medium term, but for continuity across generations it must be integrated into a larger framework of trusts, foundations, or governance mechanisms that remain intact even when the individual is no longer present.

The lesson is clear: a PoA is not architecture, but part of it. Used correctly, it is a scalpel—precise, quiet, and effective—allowing the strategist to shape outcomes without stepping into view. Used carelessly, it collapses under scrutiny, leaving both the individual and the structure exposed. Its strength is not in simplicity, but in integration—woven into a broader design that transforms temporary authority into lasting discretion.

The Signature as Presence Without Exposure

A signature is often dismissed as a formality, the final step that closes a transaction. Within Silent Power, it is far more than that. When used strategically, a signature becomes an instrument of control—proof that one can govern outcomes without titles, offices, or public roles.

The discreet strategist does not compete for visibility in registries or organizational charts. They do not seek their name in contracts, filings, or reports. Their influence rests instead in the documents that drive results. A signature executed through delegated rights, conditional powers, or private mandates can move capital, activate strategies, and shift entire corporate structures. Outsiders may never see the name behind it. Insiders know that no step moves forward without that hidden approval.

This creates a paradox: the strategist is invisible to the world yet ever-present within the system. Fiduciaries, directors, and managers all understand that their authority is contingent—that their signatures carry force only once validated by the unseen architect. Presence is constant, but it is exercised from behind the curtain.

The act of signing, in this light, is no longer an administrative step. It is a language of power. Contracts, authorizations, and private mandates become the stage where sovereignty is expressed without exposure. Authority flows through paper, not performance. Outcomes are shaped not by who stands in the spotlight, but by who controls the final word—quietly, deliberately, and unseen.

Multi-Jurisdictional Governance

One of the strategist's most advanced tools is the deliberate fragmentation of control across borders. Multi-jurisdictional governance takes what might appear fragile—dispersion—and turns it into strength. By distributing ownership, management, contracts, dispute forums, and financial flows across different legal systems, the structure itself becomes a shield. No single state has the full map. No single regulator can exert complete pressure. No single disruption can break the design.

Centralization may look efficient at first glance. Housing assets, management, and banking under one system seems simple. In reality, it concentrates risk. A single government can impose sweeping compliance rules, freeze accounts, or subject the structure to sudden political winds. A system that is visible and centralized is a system easily targeted.

Dispersed governance creates the opposite effect. A holding vehicle in Luxembourg may benefit from EU treaties. Its assets may sit under Swiss custody. Management contracts could be drafted under Singapore law. Arbitration may be routed through London or Geneva. Banking might be divided between Zurich, Dubai, and Hong Kong. To an outsider, the architecture looks complex. To the strategist, it is elegant: each jurisdiction plays a specific role, none holds the master key.

This approach is not about dodging regulation. Each component complies locally. The strength lies in compartmentalization: sovereignty preserved by design, never surrendered to one authority.

Jurisdiction Shopping Is Not Tax Evasion

The deliberate choice of jurisdictions is often misrepresented as concealment. In reality, it is legal architecture. Jurisdiction shopping means selecting the most suitable legal environment for each layer of a structure, matching law to function.

A strategist might turn to one country for fiduciary rules, another for dispute resolution, another for its banking discretion. These decisions are not illegal—they are embedded in international law and supported by the global principles of free contract, free movement, and free capital. Corporations incorporate where investor protections are strongest. Families, too, can decide where to anchor holdings, governance, or asset protection.

The aim is not opacity but resilience. A country may excel at commercial law but offer weak inheritance protections. Another may guarantee strong arbitration but limited banking privacy. Combined, they form a system that is stronger than any part alone.

For example, a family office may establish a Dutch holding to access EU frameworks. That holding's shares may sit in a Liechtenstein foundation for continuity and discretion. Swiss law may govern its strategic contracts. Financial operations may be handled in Singapore or Dubai. Regulators see what they are entitled to see, but no one sees the entire system.

The essence is intent. Jurisdiction shopping aligns obligations with strategy. It is not about evasion. It is about design.

Why Legal Dispersion Reduces Strategic Risk

A discreet structure does not survive by concentration, but by dispersal. When ownership, management, banking, and dispute resolution are distributed across jurisdictions, the system gains resilience.

If tax law changes in one country, the effect is limited to a single layer. If new disclosure rules emerge, they reveal only fragments, not the whole. If a state descends into instability, freezes assets, or exerts political pressure, the structure adapts because survival is not tied to one legal environment.

Dispersion also changes the balance of power. A regulator in one country can only demand what falls under its jurisdiction. To push further requires cooperation from other states—procedural hurdles that buy time and protect rights. What would be simple in a centralized system becomes difficult in a dispersed one.

It also forces better discipline. Boards operating under different legal traditions, assets registered under distinct systems, and contracts spread across jurisdictions require cleaner governance. Weak design risks exposure. Precision rewards resilience. In Silent Power, professionalism is part of protection.

Strategic Layering: Control, Registration, and Enforcement

One of the most refined techniques is the deliberate separation of control, registration, and enforcement. This "jurisdictional triangulation" ensures that authority is never captured from a single point.

Control may be exercised from one jurisdiction through private mandates or boards. The entity itself may be domiciled elsewhere, chosen for neutrality or favorable fiduciary law. Disputes may be routed to yet another jurisdiction—London, Geneva, or Singapore—where arbitration offers trusted enforcement.

This layering creates resilience. If one element is compromised—say, an EU directive exposes registry data in Luxembourg—the trust in Jersey or the arbitration in Switzerland remains intact. Compartmentalization prevents collapse.

Multinational corporations use the same approach. Funds may domicile in Luxembourg, administer from Ireland, and arbitrate in London. Families planning for generations adopt similar models. The aim is not needless complexity. The aim is insurance through structure.

In Silent Power, layering is not excess. It is prudence. It ensures no court, regulator, or adversary ever has the complete picture. Each part stands lawful on its own. Together, they form an architecture that is unassailable by design.

Compliance and Coordination

Running structures across several jurisdictions is never a matter of improvisation. It requires discipline, constant awareness, and an ability to anticipate. A design that looks impeccable on paper can collapse quickly if a filing is missed, a disclosure rule is misunderstood, or substance requirements are ignored. What took years to build can unravel in days, bringing penalties, audits, or reputational damage.

This is why coordination is as important as the architecture itself. Every layer must remain in harmony with the others, like instruments tuned to the same key. A holding registered in one country must align with the bank accounts that support it in another. A trust deed must be compatible with the statutes of the company it oversees. Arbitration clauses must reflect the procedural reality of the jurisdictions they invoke. If the pieces are inconsistent, adversaries—regulators, litigants, or competitors—will exploit the gaps.

No single advisor can anticipate every nuance across multiple legal systems. The strategist must therefore orchestrate counsel in each jurisdiction, ensuring that local rules are respected while the overall framework remains coherent. Anti-abuse provisions, cross-border tax rules, and reporting obligations cannot be treated reactively; they must be anticipated and absorbed into the design. What satisfies regulators in one country may raise questions in another if the internal logic is weak.

Handled correctly, this precision turns complexity into sovereignty. A structure that is fragmented yet coherent, discreet yet compliant, offers unmatched advantages: freedom to move without fear of capture, protection of identity without breach of law, and continuity of influence that survives political cycles.

Silent Power is not about avoiding rules. It is about orchestrating them—turning compliance itself into strategy, and precision into freedom.

Private Agreements vs Public Records

In Silent Power, words matter, but where they are written matters even more. A clause etched into a public register places authority under the glare of exposure. The same clause, captured in a private agreement, can carry equal or greater force while remaining unseen.

Public records exist to provide order and transparency. They name shareholders, list directors, record property, and define legal ownership. Their purpose is regulatory, but their effect is exposure. They often serve as maps for journalists, regulators, competitors, or litigants seeking to trace control.

Private agreements, by contrast, belong to the realm of enforceable but unseen law. They take the form of contracts, mandates, shareholder pacts, fiduciary deeds, or letters of wishes. Properly drafted and notarized where necessary, they carry full legal weight without ever being disclosed. They do not proclaim authority; they encode it.

The strategist's art lies in combining both systems. Public records are used to satisfy the minimum obligations–to confirm existence, legitimacy, and formal compliance. Private instruments define where true control rests, how decisions are made, who benefits, and under what conditions. On the surface, the picture is simple and often unremarkable. Beneath, private contracts preserve depth and sovereignty.

Consider a company whose registered shareholder is a fiduciary service provider. On paper, they appear as owner. Yet a sealed nominee declaration privately confirms that the rights belong elsewhere. Or picture a board of directors filled with professional names, while a shareholder pact dictates that no decision can take effect without the strategist's unseen approval. Compliance is visible, but control is concealed in the private layer.

This duality is not exotic. It is the backbone of global commerce, estate planning, and cross-border governance. The mistake many make is to treat public record as the only arena where law operates. Those who surrender to that assumption give up sovereignty the moment they sign a registry. Those who master the balance govern through contracts invisible to the public eye.

In Silent Power, authority is not only a matter of what is written. It is a matter of where it is written. The strategist understands that law speaks in two languages: one for the registry, another for the private deed. True sovereignty comes from mastering both.

The Legal Force of Private Contracts

Across nearly every modern legal system, private contracts carry binding power equal to, and sometimes exceeding, statutory provisions—so long as they rest on three foundations: mutual consent, lawful purpose, and the capacity of the parties. This deceptively simple rule forms the backbone of Silent Power. Through contracts, strategists govern what registries cannot record: the true allocation of rights, responsibilities, benefits, and control.

The reach of these instruments is immense. A shareholder pact can quietly reshape how a company is run—altering voting thresholds, embedding veto rights, or granting appointment powers that go beyond default company law. These agreements may never be published, yet they dictate the real balance of authority in boardrooms.

Silent partnerships work the same way. They allow profits to flow to participants without their names appearing in registries or public accounts. The law recognizes the arrangement, but to an outsider the beneficiary is invisible.

Mandates extend this principle further. They bind fiduciaries—nominees, trustees, or directors—to act publicly while following private instructions. These agreements form the hidden circuitry through which decisions travel, unseen in registries but fully enforceable in court.

Families add another layer with protocols that blend law with legitimacy. These documents define succession, allocate asset use, and regulate behavior across generations. They may never be filed with state authorities, yet they carry binding weight inside the family, preventing conflict and preserving continuity.

At the corporate level, service agreements between holding companies and their operating subsidiaries allocate costs, transfer risk, and define governance. These contracts, invisible to outsiders, protect internal logic and insulate strategy from public interpretation.

What unites these arrangements is discretion. They do not require publication. Unless litigation forces disclosure, they remain private, shaping outcomes without leaving obvious traces. For the strategist, contracts are not accessories—they are the primary levers of power. Public law dictates form; private agreements dictate substance. Where registries capture appearances, contracts define reality. Silent Power is exercised not in public filings but in the quiet precision of clauses that govern systems from behind the curtain.

The limitations of Public Records

Public registries were designed with clear purposes: legal certainty, administrative order, and transparency. Company registers confirm who directs a corporation. Land registries secure property rights and prevent overlapping claims. Patent and trademark databases protect intellectual property. Notarial records preserve contracts and transfers. Each system was created to promote trust and accountability.

But what makes registries useful also makes them dangerous. They expose names, dates, and links that adversaries—regulators, journalists, litigants, or competitors—can exploit. A single entry in a corporate register may reveal connections across borders. A property title may expose the scale of someone's wealth. A trademark filing may betray expansion plans before they are announced.

Recent policy shifts have increased that exposure. Beneficial ownership registers now compel individuals to disclose control behind entities. Transparency regimes force companies to submit detailed statements identifying controllers, beneficiaries, and sometimes full financials. These measures, often justified in the name of fighting crime or tax evasion, also strip away layers of privacy that once protected legitimate actors.

The unintended effect Is risk. For public figures, entrepreneurs, or families, exposure in registries can invite litigation, political pressure, reputational attacks, or even threats to safety. A tool meant to create certainty becomes a map of vulnerabilities.

For this reason, sophisticated operators treat registries with care. They disclose only what the law demands, never more. They place visible roles in the hands of fiduciaries, nominees, or purpose-built entities, while the true mechanics of control remain in private agreements: contracts, mandates, protocols, and deeds that regulators may never see unless forced by due process.

The lesson is not to reject registries. Their existence is unavoidable, and their role in law is legitimate. The strategist simply recognizes their limits. Registries establish form, not substance. They confirm existence, but they do not need to reveal direction. Silent Power accepts the surface while ensuring that control—intent, benefit, and sovereignty—remains written elsewhere, in private documents outside the public eye.

Designing the Interface Between Private and Public

Discretion is not about vanishing. It is about shaping the line between what must appear in public and what should remain hidden. The strategist accepts that certain documents—charters, registries, deeds—belong in the open. But they make sure those documents reveal only what is necessary: accurate, minimal, and compliant information, never the inner mechanics of control.

What is filed publicly is always partial. Behind it sits a deeper system of private agreements that decide how votes are cast, how assets are managed, and who holds real authority. This duality is not deception; it is the very structure of law. Legal systems themselves distinguish between formalities in public and contracts in private. Silent Power takes full advantage of that distinction.

A director may be listed in a registry as though they were in charge. In reality, their role is bound by a mandate requiring them to follow instructions from someone else. A shareholder may appear to hold equity, yet private documents dictate exactly how those shares are used or transferred. A foundation may list its board publicly, while its real governance is defined in internal bylaws never filed with state authorities.

This balance—public shell, private engine—is the essence of Silent Power. It provides legitimacy without surrendering sovereignty. The strategist remains absent from the surface yet indispensable in substance.

Resilience comes from designing this interface carefully. Those who rely only on public records hand control to the registries. Those who rely only on private contracts risk enforceability. The strategist who orchestrates both builds systems that are lawful, discreet, and unassailable.

Risk Management and Evidence

Silence is not informality. The quieter a structure, the more rigorous it must be. Contracts, mandates, and protocols that anchor invisible influence need to be drafted with precision, preserved securely, and able to withstand scrutiny in court or audit.

For that reason, evidence matters. Agreements must be signed by all relevant parties, and often notarized, legalized, or time-stamped to prove authenticity and chronology. These measures serve as anchors—quiet, but irrefutable proof that the arrangements are real and binding.

Storage is just as important. Documents must be safeguarded against tampering yet accessible when needed. Encryption, sealed notarial archives, or professional custodianship are common solutions. Silence has no value if agreements cannot be produced when challenged.

Every contract should also identify its governing law and dispute resolution forum. This is not technical detail but strategic design. A pact anchored in Swiss law, English common law, or another trusted system is not only valid but defensible across borders.

No agreement remains relevant forever. Families expand, assets change, laws evolve. Outdated contracts lose both force and protection. Updating shareholder pacts, governance protocols, and fiduciary mandates is not optional; it is essential.

Often, these private instruments operate in tandem with public filings. The registry shows the surface; the contracts show the reality. This layering ensures that while appearances satisfy regulators, substance remains defined elsewhere–silent, precise, and enforceable.

In Silent Power, evidence is not noise. It is the quiet backbone of sovereignty.

Selecting the Right People for Visible and Delegated Roles

No structure functions without people. However refined the legal design, it depends on those who occupy visible seats, act as fiduciaries, or execute delegated mandates. Choosing these individuals is one of the most delicate and decisive steps.

The wrong choice can undo years of planning. An inexperienced director may mishandle filings. A careless nominee may talk under pressure. A fiduciary with weak judgment may act opportunistically in a gray area. Documents alone cannot prevent these failures; the right actors must be in place.

The qualities that matter are competence, reliability, and alignment. Competence ensures duties are carried out without mistakes.

Reliability ensures resilience under stress—legal, financial, or reputational. Alignment means their incentives and worldview do not conflict with the strategist's design. Without these, even the most elegant structure becomes fragile.

Appointing visible figures is infrastructure, not formality. Just as an engineer chooses steel with care, the strategist must select directors, trustees, and proxies who can carry weight under pressure. They must embody restraint, respect boundaries, and remain loyal to the system rather than to circumstance.

Support and oversight matter too. Even the most trustworthy fiduciary must operate under clear mandates, defined reporting lines, and enforceable contracts. Human risk cannot be eliminated, but it can be contained. In Silent Power, trust always comes paired with structure.

Ultimately, these individuals are not decorative names. They are load-bearing pillars. Their presence upholds legitimacy in the public eye while their discretion preserves invisibility. The strategist's sovereignty depends not only on design, but on the discipline of choosing—and supervising—the right people.

Trust Is Not Enough: Profile, Background, and Compatibility

In the discipline of Silent Power, trust is a starting point, not an endpoint. Choosing fiduciaries, nominees, or visible appointees cannot be left to loyalty alone. What matters is a precise evaluation of their profile, background, and compatibility with the system. A loyal friend or relative may be dependable, but if they lack the right legal status, professional grounding, or the ability to stay calm under pressure, they can turn into liabilities far greater than the risks they were meant to absorb.

The first filter is legal status. A nominee's nationality or residence may determine whether a structure remains discreet or becomes subject to disclosure. If they are tied to high-surveillance jurisdictions, their presence could trigger reporting duties, automatic information exchange, or even unexpected tax liabilities. In such cases, the very safeguards built into the system are undermined. Jurisdictional ties, therefore, are not a detail; they are decisive.

Professional standing is the next element. Appointees who work within regulated frameworks—subject to audits, licensing, or binding codes of conduct—tend to be more disciplined and predictable. A licensed trustee, a regulated corporate services provider, or a fiduciary supervised by law will usually provide more reliability than an informal associate. In this sense, regulation is not a burden but a shield. It imposes order and makes conduct more defensible when scrutiny arises.

Reputation is equally non-negotiable. A person carrying unresolved disputes, scandals, or persistent rumors can damage the system at its first encounter with banks, regulators, or counterparties. Modern compliance systems are unforgiving; a single tarnished name can block access as effectively as a flawed contract. In Silent Power, discretion is worth more than recognition.

Then comes psychological resilience. Structures are often tested in moments of pressure: audits, litigation, hostile coverage, or political interference. A nominee who panics, improvises, or distances themselves at the wrong time can undo years of careful planning. By contrast, an appointee with composure and discipline stabilizes the system when it is most exposed. Looking at how someone has handled past crises is usually the best predictor of how they will perform under strain.

Finally, compatibility. Even the most qualified candidate must align with the architecture's intent. They need to understand the limits of their mandate, respect boundaries, and execute with precision. Overreach or improvisation corrodes the system. Compatibility means they act not as individuals in search of space, but as extensions of a design that demands discipline.

The ideal appointee is not simply trustworthy in a personal sense. They are legally sound, professionally reliable, reputationally clean, resilient under pressure, and structurally compatible. In short, they embody trust not as sentiment but as architecture. A poor choice destabilizes the entire system. The right choice becomes an invisible cornerstone of sovereignty.

Written Agreements Are Mandatory

No structure of Silent Power can rely on goodwill alone. Personal ties, however deep, do not substitute for legal clarity. Affection is not a safeguard. Without written agreements, even the most sophisticated framework risks collapsing into ambiguity or betrayal the moment discretion is most needed.

Every appointment must be formalized in writing. The agreement is not decoration–it is the architecture itself. It should spell out exactly what the appointee may do, the strict limits of their mandate, the terms of compensation if any, and the confidentiality duties binding them during and after their role. It should also detail how and under what conditions they can be replaced or removed. Precision is what transforms personal loyalty into systemic resilience.

These agreements must also contain protective clauses. Confidentiality provisions are indispensable, particularly when sensitive assets or cross-border accounts are involved. Indemnity clauses protect nominees who act within their mandate from being personally exposed to risks that belong to the structure. Dispute resolution clauses—ideally arbitration—provide a path to resolve conflicts discreetly and outside public courts.

Termination protocols are just as critical. The agreement must require the return of all documents, access codes, and powers of representation once the mandate ends. Anything left behind risks lingering exposure. Clean exits matter as much as careful entries.

Such contracts are not drafted after problems arise; they are embedded from the beginning. They are the operating manuals of Silent Power—what distinguishes informal trust from enforceable order. Without them, the system is fragile. With them, authority is not only silent, but secure.

Choosing Institutional vs. Private Fiduciaries

Every discreet structure must eventually pass through human hands. No matter how refined the design looks on paper, its execution depends on the people appointed to visible roles. At that moment, the strategist faces a decisive question: should authority be placed in the hands of an individual acting under mandate, or in those of an institution regulated to serve as fiduciary? The answer defines the structure's durability, adaptability, and discretion in real-world conditions.

Institutional fiduciaries carry the advantage of permanence. They are not tied to one person's reliability or lifespan but operate as organizations, governed by regulation and bound to continuity. Their systems—audited processes, compliance routines, internal hierarchies—ensure that mandates outlast staff changes. Many also provide indemnity coverage and bring specialized expertise in navigating cross-border compliance. For complex or long-term frameworks, this stability is invaluable. It transforms personal reliance into systemic strength.

The cost of this security Is formality. Institutional fiduciaries operate under supervision, especially in transparency-oriented jurisdictions. They must file reports, renew contracts, and meet oversight demands that can feel constraining. Their professionalism comes at a financial premium. The discreet strategist must weigh these constraints against the protection such entities provide.

Private fiduciaries, by contrast, offer speed and flexibility. Trusted associates, advisors, or family members may streamline decision-making, lower costs, and avoid bureaucratic delays. They are effective for tactical maneuvers, temporary arrangements, or situations where personal loyalty matters more than institutional weight. But they also introduce fragility. Their decisions depend on individual judgment. They may face emotional pressure or buckle under scrutiny, and when they fail, the entire system can be exposed.

The strategist's choice must always return to intent. If the architecture is meant to endure across decades, span multiple jurisdictions, or hold assets of high strategic value, institutional fiduciaries are usually the safer anchor. If the purpose is temporary, narrow in scope, or highly personal, private fiduciaries may suffice—so long as their mandate is tightly drafted and enforceable.

Convenience and cost are never the real issue. Alignment is. In Silent Power, those who occupy fiduciary roles are not mere signatories. They are structural pillars. Whether institutional or private, their appointment must reflect the deeper aim of the design: to preserve control, protect sovereignty, and ensure continuity without unnecessary exposure.

Contingency Planning: Replacing, Monitoring, and Exiting

No appointment is permanent. Even the most carefully chosen fiduciary can become a liability with time. Illness, death, regulatory pressure, shifting loyalties, or personal temptation can destabilize a role once thought secure. In Silent Power, this reality is not ignored. It is anticipated. Continuity is never left to chance—it is engineered.

From the outset, discreet structures should include mechanisms for replacement. Reserve mandates or sealed protocols designate substitutes who can step in immediately, without leaving gaps of authority or creating public transitions. These measures ensure that when one pillar fails, another is ready to carry the weight, keeping the architecture intact and unexposed.

Monitoring is equally vital. Stability cannot be assumed indefinitely. Regular reporting, contractual check-ins, or audit rights allow the strategist to detect problems early. Oversight, in this context, is not intrusive. It is quiet, consistent, and designed to identify cracks before they widen.

Emergency powers form the third safeguard. The strategist must retain the ability to revoke mandates, suspend authorities, or cut off access the moment a fiduciary begins to drift. Powers of attorney can be terminated, credentials withdrawn, and signatures blocked swiftly, preventing a local failure from spreading across the structure.

All of this must be documented. Every reserve clause, every reporting duty, every termination protocol must leave a clear legal trail, enforceable in banks, courts, and regulatory systems without requiring publicity. Continuity is not improvised; it is written into the design.

The lesson is blunt. Trust does not endure pressure. Loyalty is vulnerable to time and circumstance. What preserves sovereignty is neither sentiment nor hope, but structure. The strategist does not assume stability–they build it. Contingency planning is not optional. It is the discipline that ensures Silent Power survives when trust alone would collapse.

Building Resilient Systems of Power

The strength of Silent Power is not measured by how invisible it appears in the present but by whether it can endure over time. A structure that collapses the moment its creator withdraws is not power at all–it is fragility disguised as control. The strategist's task is to build frameworks that continue to function without constant intervention, without dependence on personal charisma, and without being bound to a single lifetime.

This demands a change in perspective. Fragile designs orbit around the individual, relying on loyalty, presence, or vigilance. Resilient designs run on their own logic. Protocols, mandates, and governance mechanisms are written in advance so that decisions, distributions, and protections follow a predetermined course, not external pressure.

Durability is therefore built into the system, not into the person. A foundation that outlives its founder, a trust that transmits intent across generations, a governance protocol that resolves disputes long after its author is gone—these are not improvised shields. They are engines of continuity. They turn temporary command into lasting sovereignty.

History provides the analogy. Empires tied to a single figure fade with that figure. Empires built on architecture endure for centuries. The same principle applies to modern structures: a family office vulnerable to succession fights will fracture, while one designed with resilient rules will carry influence forward quietly for decades.

Silent Power at its highest level is not about hiding. It is about building something that needs no defense, no spotlight, no constant reinforcement. What survives is not the architect's name but the architecture itself.

Autonomy Through Internal Rules and Triggers

Resilient systems do not wait for daily supervision. They survive because they contain their own instructions. Governance rules, succession triggers, and dispute mechanisms allow them to act without improvisation and without inviting outside interference.

A foundation offers the clearest example. Its charter can dictate who succeeds on the board, how funds are to be distributed, and under what conditions its objectives evolve. Once written, those rules govern indefinitely.

Trusts achieve the same effect through deeds and letters of wishes, embedding discretion and direction that outlast the settlor. Even holding companies can be structured to preserve continuity through supermajority voting requirements, veto rights, or escalation clauses that prevent a single hand from capturing control.

Private family protocols add yet another layer. They can be stored under seal and triggered only upon events such as incapacity or death, ensuring clarity at moments when confusion usually reigns.

Together, these rules and triggers create systems that govern themselves. The strategist no longer needs to act as a constant overseer. They become instead the author of frameworks that continue to operate in their absence. Authority shifts from personality to design.

In Silent Power, the highest control does not come from constant presence but from rules that quietly enforce intent long after the strategist has stepped aside.

Long-Term Legal Validity

Discretion without durability is an illusion. For a structure to hold, it must not only work today but remain valid in the decades ahead. This means selecting jurisdictions with tested courts, robust treaty networks, and traditions of legal stability. The goal is not to chase momentary advantages but to secure long-term predictability.

Structures built on loopholes collapse when the loopholes close. Those built on stable legal traditions endure reforms, shifts in political climate, and regulatory waves. Compliance, therefore, is not an obstacle to Silent Power but one of its foundations. Substance rules, anti-abuse measures, and cross-border tax regulations must be anticipated at the design stage.

Coherence is equally important. The purpose of the structure must be lawful, its functions real, and its documents aligned. Fragile arrangements fail not because they are hidden but because they cannot be defended. What survives are systems that are consistent and intelligible under scrutiny, even when they remain discreet in practice.

The lesson is straightforward. Silence without substance will not last. But design that matches reality—lawful, coherent, and strategic—creates resilience. Silent Power is not about stepping outside the law; it is about embedding sovereignty within it.

Human Succession and Knowledge Transfer

Even the most sophisticated legal design cannot stand on documents alone. Continuity depends on people who will one day assume roles within the structure, whether visible or hidden. Succession, in this context, is not about naming heirs openly. It is about ensuring that knowledge and discipline are transferred without exposing the architecture before its time.

Information should be revealed in layers: sealed letters, memoranda, or protocols released only under triggers such as incapacity or death. Training of successors is equally critical. They must learn not just the technical mechanics but the culture of discretion—the ability to operate without noise, to think in compartments, and to act with discipline.

Trusted advisors—lawyers, fiduciaries, or long-standing consultants—often serve as bridges, carrying institutional memory and ensuring continuity through generational shifts or jurisdictional changes.

What succession truly preserves is not a title but a system. Names fade; rules endure. The strategist's achievement is not to hold power visibly, but to design it so that it continues to operate without them. Silent Power achieves permanence not at the level of the individual, but at the level of architecture.

Enduring Power Is Invisible, Not Absent

From the outside, resilient structures often look self-sufficient. Boards hold meetings, trustees carry out instructions, contracts unfold, and everything appears to move on its own. Yet this impression of independence is misleading. What actually drives the system is a coded design—rules, mandates, and triggers embedded long before—that ensures continuity without requiring the constant hand of its creator.

This is not a withdrawal from leadership. It is leadership in its most advanced form. The strategist does not cling to formal positions, signatures, or constant visibility. Instead, authority is built into the system itself. Once written into statutes, protocols, and governance frameworks, it survives without the need for its author to remain on stage.

The strength of Silent Power lies precisely in this shift from presence to design. Authority no longer depends on personality; it rests in structures that act consistently, silently, and with legitimacy. In that silence, power is not diminished. It becomes harder to attack, less dependent on circumstance, and capable of enduring across generations.

Statutes, contracts, sealed directives, and carefully chosen fiduciaries do more than manage wealth. They transmit intent without exposure. They protect sovereignty without spectacle. They allow decisions to be enforced without noise. In doing so, they speak more clearly and more durably than any public declaration.

Lasting power is therefore not absent—it is hidden in plain sight, woven into systems that function without fanfare. The architect may step away, even vanish entirely, yet the design continues to guide outcomes. Visible power fades when its holder disappears. Invisible power persists because it has been written into the architecture itself.

Final Note - Control Is Not About Ego, But Design

The central lesson is stark: control is not measured by presence or recognition, but by design. True power does not rely on applause, titles, or headlines. It rests on frameworks that work regardless of who is visible, rules that remain after personalities fade, and mechanisms that decide outcomes without drawing attention.

In a world that celebrates exposure, sovereignty often survives only beneath the surface. The silent strategist knows that it is not necessary to appear as a director, a founder, or a public figure. What matters is constructing positions that guide without being seen, contracts that bind without being public, and systems that continue to function long after the author has stepped aside.

This chapter has traced the instruments of invisible authority: nominees that provide form without substance, delegated signatures that separate action from exposure, multi-jurisdictional governance that disperses risk, private agreements that define reality outside registries, and resilience mechanisms that give permanence to fragile designs. Each of these tools shows that Silent Power is not about improvisation. It is a deliberate architecture—lawful, coherent, and stable.

The danger lies not in external pressure but in ego. When control depends on recognition or visibility, it loses strength. Structures built on personality rather than design collapse under scrutiny. What endures is restraint: allowing frameworks to govern, letting contracts and statutes carry intent, and accepting invisibility as the price of permanence.

Silent Power is more real because it does not need to be seen. Its strength lies in not asking for confirmation. Its continuity comes not from reputation but from design.

With this foundation in place, the next step is practice: how to operate inside these systems, how to move across borders, and how to cultivate mobility while staying discreet, effective, and fully legal.

CHAPTER IV - THE ART OF INVISIBLE LIVING

Invisibility Is Not Disappearance

To be invisible does not mean to vanish. It is not retreat, nor abdication. It is the ability to remain present without creating disturbance, to shape outcomes without leaving fingerprints, to move through the world without generating signals that call for attention.

Earlier chapters laid out the legal and structural mechanics of Silent Power. This one turns to the human side: the habits, choices, and disciplines that make discretion a lived reality rather than a technical design.

Many structures fail not because the documents are weak, but because the lives behind them contradict the architecture. A person may set up holding companies with careful layers of protection, then announce their movements online. They may establish trusts for long-term stability, yet cultivate a lifestyle so conspicuous that it negates the very purpose of those vehicles. They pursue invisibility on paper while embracing the performance culture of social media. What looks solid collapses under the weight of inconsistency.

Silent living requires alignment between structure and conduct. It is not simply about staying off the radar; it is about arranging life so that every signal—residence, travel, communication, even the way one interacts socially—remains consistent with the principle of discretion. It is the practice of producing no unnecessary noise. Movement flows without drawing lawsuits, political interference, or envy.

This chapter examines the craft of lifestyle engineering: how to select residences that balance privacy and access, how to travel without leaving a trail of visibility, how to communicate without leakage, how to invest without spectacle, and how to manage social and professional relations in ways that reinforce freedom instead of compromising it.

Invisible living is not withdrawal. It is not exile or denial. It is elegance stripped of vanity, presence without performance. It is the life of someone whose influence works quietly, continuously, and beyond reach—someone who does not need to be seen to matter.

Designing a Lifestyle That Doesn't Invite Noise

To live powerfully yet discreetly, one must start with the ground level: daily life. Legal structures can shield, but they become fragile when the person behind them sends signals that attract attention. Silent Power is not upheld by documents alone; it is strengthened—or undone—by how one lives, moves, and appears.

For the strategist, lifestyle is not random. It is curated. Every choice—residence, dress, transportation, digital presence—is intentional. The aim is not withdrawal from life but mastery over its projection.

Where traditional wealth often announces itself with noise and display, silent power takes the opposite approach. Its aesthetic is quiet, understated, deliberate. It does not invite curiosity; it does not provoke interference. The point is not to deny enjoyment, but to avoid the trap of spectacle.

The first discipline is to understand that lifestyle is never neutral. Where one lives sends a message to banks and tax authorities. How one dresses communicates status and alignment. Cars, homes, photographs, and posts each tell a story. Those stories are read not just by regulators or journalists, but by acquaintances, competitors, and algorithms scanning for patterns.

The question is not whether signals are sent—they always are. The question is what narrative they build, and whether that narrative is shaped intentionally or left to chance. The discreet strategist ensures that signals are muted, neutral, or redirected. The story projected outward is one of stability, reliability, and normality. Real power operates elsewhere, quietly, untraceable.

Silent Power begins with the smallest of daily decisions. A curated lifestyle is not vanity. It is a defense, a language of elegance, and an expression of sovereignty.

The Myth of Luxury Visibility

Modern culture feeds a dangerous illusion: that wealth must be displayed to be respected. From advertising campaigns to curated feeds, from glossy real estate showcases to influencers staging their lives online, the message repeats itself—visibility equals success. For those who care about continuity, privacy, and real influence, this equation is false. Visibility is not respect. It is risk.

There is nothing wrong with enjoying wealth. Comfort, refinement, and beauty are legitimate pursuits. What corrodes discretion is not the enjoyment itself but the urge to perform it. The parade of possessions, the endless posting, the insistence on display often reveal not confidence but insecurity—a need for validation that undermines sovereignty.

True wealth cannot be captured by symbols. It is freedom—the ability to move without restriction. It is control—the power to arrange one's affairs without interference. It is continuity—the assurance that what is built endures across generations, insulated from volatility and reputation. None of this is secured by likes, mentions, or the illusion of belonging to visible circles.

Silent living does not renounce quality. It redefines how quality is expressed. A tailored suit without logos radiates refinement without announcing affiliation. A high-performance vehicle in muted tones offers mastery without spectacle. A property held through a discreet structure provides stability and access without putting its owner's name in lights.

In this logic, luxury stops being performance and becomes internal. It is measured in states of being: peace of mind, control, the ability to move unbothered through a noisy world. For the strategist, the highest luxury is not to be noticed, but to be free.

Wealth Signaling vs. Wealth Shielding

Wealth always produces signals. A car, an address, a watch, even a photograph—each becomes a marker of status or belonging. To signal wealth is to use these markers deliberately, showing affluence to communicate success. In some fields this is functional: a gallerist who collects art, a politician who demonstrates reach, a broker whose credibility depends on displaying lifestyle. There, signaling serves as currency.

In the world of discretion, however, signaling is costly. Every display carries a price. A photo with a politician might impress certain audiences, but it also places the strategist's name in compliance files, intelligence reports, or reputational maps. A brightly colored car may invite admiration, but also audits, surveillance, theft, or envy. A luxury home in a famous enclave brings prestige—and a fixed target for litigants or journalists.

The strategist's question is simple: what does this signal cost me, not in money but in exposure? Each gesture invites more eyes. Some will flatter. Others will probe. The benefits are uncertain. The risk accumulates.

Shielding is the opposite discipline. It does not deny wealth but strips away unnecessary signals. Shielding means living in ways that keep patterns indistinguishable from ordinary professionals, avoiding predictable jurisdictions, and projecting a surface of stability rather than extravagance. It is the art of remaining unreadable.

A home can be luxurious, but layered through entities that conceal ownership. A vehicle can be powerful, but understated. A bank account may manage millions, but with outward behavior indistinguishable from that of a middle-class executive. Shielding does not reduce access to quality. It reduces vulnerability.

Signaling makes one a target. Shielding makes one untraceable. In a culture obsessed with visibility, the quiet path is not deprivation—it is freedom.

Choosing Environments That Reinforce Discretion

Environment is never neutral. It is the filter through which every signal and every gesture is interpreted. The same lifestyle that blends unnoticed in Geneva can appear ostentatious in Marbella. What passes without comment in Singapore may stand out as unusual in Lisbon. Visibility is relative. Context decides whether you are background or spectacle.

Three dimensions define a discreet environment. The first is cultural. Some societies treat privacy as a boundary. Asking personal questions is impolite; wealth is not a topic for gossip. In others, curiosity is constant, and visibility is demanded by social custom. Choosing where to live is therefore not only about climate or taxes but about whether culture allows one to exist without constant explanation.

The second dimension is regulatory. Jurisdictions with predictable rules and tested institutions provide protection. They turn compliance into routine rather than confrontation. Environments where laws shift suddenly, or where enforcement bends to headlines, expose even the most careful strategist.

The third dimension is social. Certain circles—diplomatic networks, legacy families, academic and legal environments—value silence and restraint above display. Within them, discretion is etiquette. Presence is not performance.

Selecting such environments does not mean exile or austerity. It means choosing spaces that do not force justification, where privacy is not an oddity but a given. In those contexts, freedom comes not from hiding, but from not needing to explain.

Designing a lifestyle that avoids noise is not concealment. It is the discipline of refusing to create unnecessary narratives. The closer the alignment between environment and intent, the less correction will ever be required.

Power is not built by silence alone. It is built by living in places where silence is natural, expected, and respected.

Mobility Without Trace: Smart Travel and Residency

In the twenty-first century, mobility is both privilege and hazard. It opens access to markets, cultures, and networks, yet each border crossed produces data. Passports are scanned into shared systems, immigration logs accumulate, and even the simplest action—using a local SIM card or swiping a credit card abroad—extends a trail that can later be reconstructed. The discreet strategist does not resist this reality. They shape it, turning movement into a calibrated instrument: global, fluid, and active, yet without scattering signals that invite scrutiny.

Travel today is not only about tickets and visas. It is about residency rights, tax thresholds, and jurisdictional footprints. Every night spent in a territory can be counted toward residency claims. Every landing may trigger reporting duties under international information-sharing regimes. Mobility therefore demands precision. It is not a matter of constant movement, nor of avoiding borders, but of orchestrating presence so that no single jurisdiction acquires undue control.

Residency itself has evolved into a strategic asset. Investor programs, second residencies, and non-domicile regimes grant both access and optionality. When embedded into broader structures, they allow the strategist to function across geographies without being captured by any of them. The aim is never evasion. It is configuration: structuring presence so that it remains lawful, coherent, and chosen rather than imposed.

Mobility without trace does not mean disappearance. It means moving so that presence remains clear to the strategist yet opaque to outsiders. It is the discipline of ensuring that data, location, and rights serve the design, not compromise it. Travel is deliberate. Residency is intentional. Movement itself becomes a language—speaking volumes to those who matter, and silence to everyone else.

Second Residencies and Visa-Free Corridors

Depending on a single passport or residency is a form of captivity. It ties sovereignty to one state, exposing the individual to sudden reforms, political turbulence, or administrative overreach. For the discreet strategist, multiple residencies are not a hedge born of fear but an act of foresight. They provide flexibility—the cornerstone of discretion.

A second residency does not need to be a second home. It is an option, a legal foothold, a right of entry that avoids automatic fiscal or social entanglements. Calibration is key: the right to stay without the obligation to become anchored.

Smart mobility begins with the corridors that connect systems seamlessly. EU long-term residents move through Schengen with minimal friction. Caribbean residencies or citizenships unlock entry into the United Kingdom or Commonwealth states while, if carefully structured, remaining outside certain reporting regimes. Singaporean or Emirati residencies open vast networks of travel and commerce without attaching heavy global taxation.

But access must never be confused with attachment. A property abroad does not in itself establish residence. Only when time, intent, and use converge do fiscal or regulatory ties arise. The strategist learns to separate entry rights from legal obligations—knowing precisely what each stay, each stamp, each record silently registers.

Residencies are collected not for prestige but for optionality. Passports are valued not for symbolism but for the doors they open. The measure is always sovereignty: movement without entanglement, presence without captivity.

Digital Footprints While Moving Across Borders

Crossing borders today is not merely physical. Every traveler carries an invisible convoy of devices and data—phones, laptops, tablets, cloud accounts—that often reveal more than the passport in hand. In many jurisdictions, border agents can inspect these devices without warrant. What was once a simple stamp can become a probe into emails, files, or encrypted chats. For the strategist, digital discretion begins before departure.

The disciplined traveler minimizes exposure by using secondary devices configured with limited information, stripped of sensitive archives, and secured with encrypted tools that do not automatically synchronize with the cloud. Some rely on air-gapped machines or remote desktops hosted in secure jurisdictions, ensuring that the hardware carried across borders is a shell, not the system itself.

Yet digital trails extend far beyond the devices. Airline manifests, hotel check-ins, ride-share apps, and card transactions build timelines more revealing than a passport. These patterns, while lawful, map associations, spending habits, and routines that can later be mined for leverage.

The aim is not to abandon technology but to mute unnecessary visibility. Cash may replace cards in certain contexts. Walkable cities or private drivers reduce the digital residue of daily movement. What looks old-fashioned is in fact strategic: fewer records, fewer narratives, less exposure.

In Silent Power, travel is never random. Crossing borders is as much about information control as it is about geography. The discreet strategist ensures that the story told by their movements is no story at all—neutral, unremarkable, and undeserving of attention.

When and Where to Declare (or Not Declare) Presence

In the discipline of Silent Power, presence is never neutral. To appear somewhere—whether physically, legally, or fiscally—activates consequences. Some are immediate, others unfold quietly over time. Declaring presence can be advantageous, but often it is optional. The strategist's role is to distinguish between the two and act with precision.

Residency standards vary widely. Many states apply the well-known 183-day rule, measuring presence in days. Others focus on the center of vital interests: where family, assets, or economic activity are concentrated. Aggressive jurisdictions such as Spain, France, or the United States interpret residence broadly, attaching it to habitual presence, property access, or even family ties. By contrast, regimes like Portugal's non-domicile system, Malta's residence-by-investment programs, or the UAE's permits create more flexible frameworks, activating obligations only when formally invoked or used.

These distinctions are not academic. A declaration in one jurisdiction may open the door to tax duties, reporting obligations, or compliance risks that ripple across the entire structure. In another, the same declaration can be beneficial, securing treaty access, institutional credibility, or tax neutrality. The strategist does not reject residency altogether; they select it deliberately, choosing those jurisdictions that strengthen rather than weaken the design.

Every decision about presence must be tested through three filters:

- Will declaring here trigger obligations that bind me beyond intent?

- Does this residency reinforce the structure, or compromise it?
- Am I adding value—or merely visibility—by being here?

These are not abstractions. A U.S. Green Card grants mobility, yet it also imposes lifelong tax reporting. Swiss residence offers stability and prestige, but only if paired with carefully negotiated taxation. UAE residency provides neutrality, though it requires minimal physical presence to retain validity.

Discretion in mobility is not about hiding. It is about recognizing that every step, stamp, or declaration has consequences. Sovereignty lies in ensuring those consequences serve the architecture rather than erode it.

Discreet Communication and Digital Hygiene

Breakdowns in discretion rarely begin with financial leaks or legal flaws. More often, they start with words. In today's environment, every call is logged, every message indexed, every click archived. What was once fleeting—a note, a phone conversation—is now permanent. Influence requires communication, but communication creates evidence.

The strategist approaches this paradox with discipline. Digital hygiene is not paranoia; it is prudence. Sensitive instructions are never left lingering in systems that can be intercepted, duplicated, or misinterpreted. What undermines carefully built structures is not law but carelessness in speech.

Discreet communication does not mean secrecy for secrecy's sake. It means controlling access to thought and intent. A single email or text reveals more than content: it discloses timing, tone, relationships, and behavioral patterns. Once transmitted, it no longer belongs to you. Encryption may secure delivery, but it cannot prevent misuse by the recipient, nor can it erase metadata that shows when, where, and with whom the exchange occurred.

The strategist therefore minimizes, compartmentalizes, and neutralizes. They reduce what is written. They separate conversations by platform, geography, and role so that no leak can reveal the entire picture. And they strip messages of unnecessary context, ensuring that even if exposed, they do not compromise the architecture.

In Silent Power, sovereignty extends to language itself. What is not said is often more decisive than what is declared.

Devices, Metadata, and the Illusion of Privacy

Encrypted apps promise security, but they protect only content. They do not shield the metadata: who spoke, when, how often, and for how long. These patterns expose hierarchies, rhythms, and intent. Investigators, regulators, and litigators know this, which is why they pursue logs as aggressively as messages.

For the strategist, every connected device is a potential liability. A phone that mixes personal life with strategic matters creates a unified trail—easy to map, easy to exploit.

Mitigation requires foresight. Travel phones configured with minimal data, reset or discarded after use. Air-gapped devices for sensitive matters, never connected to public networks. Virtual desktops hosted in secure jurisdictions, leaving nothing stored locally. These are not extravagances; they are modern equivalents of safes and vaults.

Digital trails also extend beyond devices. Hotel check-ins, flight manifests, ride-sharing apps, and payment records together reconstruct entire itineraries. The aim is not to avoid technology but to prevent unnecessary records. Cash, private transport, or deliberately "inconvenient" methods often provide the most effective safeguards.

What emerges is control, not paranoia. Privacy is not assumed—it is engineered. In Silent Power, the strategist ensures that what metadata can reveal is as carefully shaped as the content itself.

Clean Channels for Sensitive Discussions

Every conversation has a level of sensitivity. Casual talk can occur anywhere. Operational, legal, or strategic exchanges cannot. The discreet strategist assigns each to its proper channel.

Confidential matters are never left to general-purpose platforms, however encrypted. They are conducted in secure environments, often through devices reserved exclusively for that role. Segregation is key: one phone for logistics, another for strategy. One archive for routine matters, another for sealed protocols.

Sometimes the most effective safeguard is the least technical: simplicity. In-person dialogue, handwritten notes, or oral exchanges conducted without devices may be inconvenient, yet they leave no audit trail. In an era that values speed and convenience, inconvenience itself becomes protection.

Even when digital tools are necessary, the strategist thinks beyond transmission. The risk is not only in what is said, but in how it is stored, copied, or misused later. Platforms cannot be trusted blindly. Nor can people. The safeguard is design: agreements, habits, and protocols that ensure exposure is minimized before it arises.

Discretion in communication is not silence—it is sovereignty over speech.

Behavioral Patterns That Reveal More Than Data

Surveillance is not always about technology. More often, it takes shape in behavior. The rhythm of communication—when you respond, whom you ignore, when you are always reachable, and when you remain silent—forms a signature of its own. These patterns can expose priorities, discipline, and vulnerabilities more clearly than any intercepted message.

The way a person communicates reflects the way they think. Those who reply impulsively, overshare, or allow emotion to dictate their words leave trails of inconsistency. Those who respond with deliberation, compartmentalize exchanges, and keep messages factual create resilience. Silence, when intentional, is not absence; it is strategy.

The strategist trains themselves to communicate as though they were designing a structure: neutral, modular, and deliberate. Every word is crafted to stand alone, able to be read by outsiders—whether through accident, coercion, or design—without dismantling the larger system. Speaking as though every sentence may one day be published is not paranoia. It is armor.

Invisibility, then, is not only about moving quietly but about speaking with precision—or choosing not to speak at all. Some of the strongest influence is exercised in silence. And when words are used, the timing, tone, and context matter as much as the content.

Communication, when handled with discipline, becomes part of the architecture of Silent Power. Nothing is improvised; everything is shaped with intent.

Managing Wealth Without Flash

Wealth has always been a form of power, but in the modern world its strength depends less on accumulation than on protection. In an era where banks share records across borders, where ownership registries are searchable with ease, and where every transaction leaves a digital imprint, capital is no longer private by default. The greatest threat to wealth today is not volatility—it is visibility.

Markets can be hedged, diversified, or managed. What cannot be reversed is exposure: when assets become legible to too many eyes, when balance sheets turn into dossiers, when fortunes meant to shield instead become targets. For the strategist, the objective is not concealment for its own sake but structure—arranging prosperity so it cannot be profiled, frozen, or turned into leverage by regulators, litigants, or rivals.

To manage wealth without flash is not to retreat. It is to refine expression. Well-managed wealth does not shout; it sustains. It provides liquidity without parading bank statements, preserves continuity without igniting inheritance disputes, and creates influence without demanding visibility.

The confusion lies in equating display with security. Many mistake luxury signals for credibility, visibility for validation, or publicity for permanence. Yet history is filled with fortunes destroyed because they were too visible, too traceable, too vulnerable to envy and appetite. Silent

Power teaches the opposite lesson: wealth is secure only when its architecture prevents it from becoming a target.

The strategist who manages wealth discreetly is not poorer but freer. Their prosperity is measured not in symbols but in sovereignty—the ability to decide how, where, and to what extent their resources are seen or used. Those who fail to recognize this distinction often lose both the appearance and the substance of wealth.

How the Ultra-Wealthy Operate Quietly

Public imagination insists that the richest people are those whose names appear on magazine covers, billionaire rankings, or curated global lists. Reality often works in reverse. Many of the most powerful individuals are precisely those who remain absent from these registers. Their invisibility is not lack of status; it is protection.

They rarely own anything directly. Real estate is layered through holding companies scattered across jurisdictions. Corporate stakes sit under fiduciaries or trustees bound by private agreements. Intellectual property, often the most valuable of modern assets, is lodged in foundations that preserve continuity while concealing attribution. The design is deliberate, layered, and resistant to mapping.

Their enjoyment of luxury follows the same logic. It is not abstention but discretion. Yachts sail under special-purpose vehicles. Aircraft are leased rather than owned. Villas are used through holding entities or long-term contracts. Public records show nothing that links their names to the assets they enjoy. Lifestyle never becomes liability.

Just as significant are the actions they avoid. They seldom pursue public listings, headline-grabbing political donations, or flamboyant speculative plays—activities that attract scrutiny and erode discretion. Their influence flows instead through intermediaries, private councils, and closed networks where visibility is neither required nor useful.

The lesson is clear. Visibility is not the price of success; it is often the cost of losing control. Those who chase acknowledgment in rankings or headlines trade sovereignty for exposure. Those who understand Silent Power measure prosperity not in applause, but in the degree to which they can move, invest, and decide without interference.

Financial Habits of Discreet Families

Enduring prosperity rarely comes from sudden windfalls. It is usually generational, designed to survive transitions in power, markets, and even political climates. It is wealth managed for continuity rather than applause. To outsiders, the practices of such families may appear conservative, almost restrained. In reality, this restraint conceals a refined discipline—habits that protect sovereignty and preserve influence across decades.

These families view private banks not as trophies, but as instruments of stability and continuity. Loyalty is built through long-term relationships rather than short-term returns. A banker who understands the family's architecture deeply is less likely to make errors that expose it. For them, institutional memory is not sentimental—it is strategic insurance.

They avoid unnecessary leverage. Debt is seen less as a tool for growth than as a potential point of vulnerability. Instead, capital is structured with caution, diversified across vehicles, and housed in jurisdictions chosen for legal resilience as much as for fiscal efficiency.

Their spending habits are intentionally quiet. They avoid purchases that generate volatility in their financial profile or unnecessary attention in the public eye. Art is acquired but stored in freeports or vaults, where it appreciates without spectacle. Properties are held through legal vehicles rather than personal title, ensuring that enjoyment never becomes exposure. Even philanthropy is managed with discretion: gifts flow through foundations or umbrella funds, often anonymously, so that impact is preserved without entangling the family in political or reputational narratives.

This is not fear-driven behavior. It is the pursuit of freedom—the freedom to operate without intrusive inquiries, to avoid litigation traps, to live without envy distorting perception, and to resist institutional overreach. Their wealth is measured not in symbols but in security, not in display but in continuity. The lesson is simple: prosperity that endures is never loud.

Leveraging Private Banks Without Attracting Attention

Private banking is powerful, but only when handled with discipline. The mistake many make is confusing it with prestige—treating the brand, the lobbies, and the invitations as signs of security. A bank is not a status symbol; it is a tool. Its value lies in its configuration, not in its appearance.

The strategist selects institutions based on discretion, cross-border expertise, and resilience. The right bank offers multi-jurisdictional custody, legal advisory strength, and deep compliance competence. Accounts are rarely in personal names unless required. Instead, they are held through entities—trusts, foundations, or holding companies—that build distance between individual and capital. Mandates are limited, powers of attorney are reviewed and revoked when needed, and communication flows formally through counsel.

Risk is never concentrated. No matter how discreet, no single bank is allowed full visibility. Custody is spread, jurisdictions alternated, reporting mapped with precision. This ensures that no one institution or authority can claim control. Even banker relationships are handled with formality. Familiarity never substitutes for documentation. Instructions are recorded, staff changes monitored, and boundaries kept clear.

In this framework, wealth management is not performance–it is precision. The goal is not to be admired by the institution but to remain untouchable within it.

Networks, Relationships, and Strategic Silence

Power is never exercised in isolation. Every strategist, however discreet, operates through networks–of advisors, intermediaries, and silent facilitators. Behind every enduring structure lies a web of relationships that carries influence, access, and capital. The question is not whether networks exist, but how they are designed.

Relationships are treated as assets, subject to the same discipline as financial holdings. Each conversation, introduction, or association carries potential consequences. A misplaced confidence may outlast a financial loss. The strategist curates rather than collects, surrounding themselves with allies who share values of discipline, confidentiality, and long-term vision.

At the heart of this lies strategic silence. Silence is not avoidance; it is a decision about presence. Sometimes absence speaks louder than attendance. Sometimes restraint carries more weight than comment.

Silence allows influence to flow through intermediaries, through proxies, through logic encoded into systems, without exposure.

In this way, networks cease to be webs of noise. They become frameworks of sovereignty—quiet, precise, and resilient.

Building Influence Without Building Noise

Contemporary culture confuses noise with influence. The loudest voices are assumed to hold authority. In practice, real influence often leaves no trace. It is exercised not through volume, but through structure. The strategist does not compete for attention. They design the environment in which others act.

This influence grows in spaces without cameras or transcripts, in conversations that are remembered but not recorded. It builds on trust, not on followers, and flourishes where loyalty matters more than performance.

To build influence without noise requires precision. It means cultivating credibility with the few rather than seeking attention from the many. It means providing value so consistently that absence becomes disruptive, that withdrawal shapes outcomes more than presence. Silence itself becomes leverage, ensuring the strategist's hand directs without ever appearing.

In this model, the individual does not become the message. They become the architecture. Their strength is not in being seen but in ensuring that everything around them moves in line with their design. Influence that is visible fades with the cycle of attention. Influence that is silent endures.

When to Speak, and When Silence Is the True Signal

Words carry weight. A single statement can move markets, sway a negotiation, or shift the course of a dispute. Yet in the practice of Silent Power, restraint often carries more force than expression. Every word is a signal—of intent, alignment, or weakness. Once released, it cannot be retrieved. The strategist's discipline lies not only in choosing what to say, but in deciding whether to speak at all.

They rarely speak without purpose. They do not rush to explain or defend. Instead, they let silence work in their favor, creating uncertainty and prompting others to reveal themselves. Far from diminishing influence, withholding words amplifies it. Silence unsettles, leaving space that others feel compelled to fill, often exposing more than they intended.

There are moments when words cannot be avoided—litigation, crisis response, critical negotiations. In those cases, speech must be exact, pared down to what is essential, and free of unnecessary emotion. Each word functions as a scalpel, closing doors rather than opening them. Influence here does not come from volume but from clarity.

Most of the time, however, silence remains the stronger posture. It prevents overexposure, compels others to speak first, and preserves options that premature declarations would foreclose. In diplomacy, silence is often read as authority. In business, it creates leverage. In personal power, it signals control. Speech is finite. Silence is endless. And within that infinity lies sovereignty.

The Role of Trusted Intermediaries

No strategist operates alone. Influence flows through people as well as structures. The question is never whether intermediaries will speak, but who speaks, when, and under what limits. Lawyers, fiduciaries, diplomats, and advisors serve as filters—projecting presence while preserving distance. Their value lies in absorbing pressure, deflecting attention, and keeping the strategist outside the noise.

An intermediary who seeks credit is a liability. Their role is not to claim authority but to shield it. They may appear at a negotiation table, but they never speculate on intent. They may be quoted, but their words never reveal the true design. They are conduits, not actors.

Trust in such figures cannot be improvised. It is tested over time, measured in their response to stress and their ability to remain within boundaries. Contracts define their scope, but discipline defines their reliability. The strategist ensures that incentives are aligned, authority is limited, and loyalty is not assumed but observed.

In this way, intermediaries become more than assistants—they become firewalls. When sound must be made, it comes from them, filtered and detached, leaving the strategist untouched.

Living Authentically Without Leaving Traces

Invisibility does not mean suppression. It is not disguise or denial of self. The higher form of Silent Power lies in living authentically while leaving no unnecessary record. What is most meaningful does not demand public validation. It exists without display.

Authenticity here is private, not performative. It does not require applause, nor does it depend on constant affirmation. The strategist's identity is aligned within, not negotiated in the marketplace of opinion. They are present where it matters, absent where visibility adds nothing.

To outsiders, such a life may appear enigmatic. Yet it is deeply coherent. It is lived without the compulsion to narrate, without the burden of proof for strangers. Freed from performance, energy is directed to substance—relationships that endure, work that matters, experiences that nourish. In this, authenticity becomes a private anchor, not a public statement.

Invisible living does not diminish richness. It enhances it. By refusing to turn life into content, the strategist protects both meaning and sovereignty.

Purpose Without Performance

Contemporary culture confuses purpose with publicity. Careers are staged on LinkedIn, convictions broadcast on social feeds, family lives curated for strangers. What passes for meaning is often reduced to content. Purpose becomes fragile when it depends on the gaze of others, for the same audience that validates it today can dismantle it tomorrow.

The silently powerful follow another path. Their purpose does not require visibility. It is inward-facing, steady, and resilient. They measure their legacy in continuity, not applause. Their fulfillment lies in alignment, not recognition. Because their purpose is not performed, it does not collapse when fashions change or when narratives fade.

Purpose for them is not a slogan. It is an operating principle. It guides decisions, sets boundaries, and determines when to speak and when to remain silent. Anchored internally, it does not need defense, nor does it bend to misinterpretation.

This is not withdrawal. It is sovereignty. A purpose that is lived rather than performed cannot be stripped away. It survives beyond audience, beyond reputation, beyond noise.

Legacy Over Lifestyle

Lifestyle and legacy are often confused, but they belong to different worlds. Lifestyle can be purchased, displayed, and discarded. It is fragile, tied to taste, markets, and fashion. It appears quickly, fades just as fast, and leaves little once the spotlight moves elsewhere. Legacy, by contrast, cannot be bought, photographed, or staged. It is designed, structured, and preserved. Lifestyle is performance. Legacy is architecture.

To live invisibly yet authentically is to place energy not in what advertises you, but in what outlives you. Legacy takes many shapes: a foundation that endures beyond its founder, a body of work that continues to shape thought, an architecture that sustains continuity across generations, or a circle of protégés who carry forward a philosophy without needing to cite its source. Legacy can also be subtler: the quiet reshaping of a market, the seeding of ideas whose influence survives long after names are forgotten, or the introduction of norms that permanently shift how societies operate.

True legacy is not ego projected into the future. It is the culmination of discipline and design. It requires building systems that endure, entrusting them to the right custodians, and accepting that the strongest influence is often detached from its author. To disappear from outcomes you engineered is not to lose recognition—it is the highest proof of control.

This is the final refinement of Silent Power: to ensure continuity not because it bears your name, but because it was built strong enough to stand alone. Legacy is not the echo of performance. It is the persistence of design. And in silence, it becomes permanent.

Peace as the Ultimate Asset

In a world defined by volatility and speed, peace is not weakness. It is strength in its purest form. Not passivity, but sovereignty. Peace is the ability to sleep without fear, to act without hunger for credit, and to move without resistance. It is the quiet condition in which nothing essential can be taken, because everything that matters has already been secured.

Peace cannot be purchased or staged. It can only be earned–through disciplined structure, foresight in design, and restraint in expression. It emerges when wealth no longer dictates identity, when presence no longer requires performance, and when purpose no longer bends to validation.

Those who master invisible living are not fugitives. They are not hiding. They are choosing. They prioritize endurance over entertainment, sovereignty over spectacle, legacy over lifestyle. They do not reject the world; they redesign their place within it. They construct meaning, protection, and impact that operate without noise.

To live authentically without leaving traces is not to erase yourself from history. It is to write history on your own terms–deciding what is visible, to whom, and when. It is authorship without exposure, influence without dependence, presence without demand.

This is Silent Power at its highest refinement: a life where peace itself becomes the ultimate asset—untouchable, untraded, and undiminished, anchored in the sovereignty of silence.

Final Reflection: Privacy Is Power, But Only if Lived Consistently

Invisible living is not a collection of tricks to avoid scrutiny. It is not a tactic. It is a philosophy of sovereignty, and like all philosophies, it begins within. It does not start with structures or passports, but with clarity: What do you value? What do you intend to protect? What kind of life are you willing to build slowly, without showing it to anyone?

Across borders and generations, those who practice Silent Power share the same discipline. They treat time, energy, and information as sacred resources—never wasted, never performed, never surrendered for applause. They do not rush to post, declare, or defend. They build frameworks that guard them, and they cultivate behaviors that never contradict the architecture they designed.

This chapter traced the human dimension of discretion: the emotional, logistical, and strategic habits that transform privacy into lived practice. Yet it is not a checklist—it is a mirror. What it reflects is personal. Each individual must define their balance between visibility and silence, between movement and anchoring, between voice and restraint.

Strategies differ. Some will focus on building legacies, others on protecting what already exists. Some will optimize for peace, others for preparedness. Some will pursue beauty, others safety, others creation. Each path is valid, so long as it is coherent, deliberate, and silent where it must be.

Discretion is not hiding. It is the ability to decide precisely where to be seen—and to leave the rest untraceable. Here lies the paradox of Silent Power: the less that is visible, the more that endures.

CHAPTER V - DIGITAL SILENCE: CYBER HYGIENE FOR THE ELITE

Why Silent Power Demands Digital Precision

In earlier generations, discretion was largely a matter of paper and presence. Risks were born of misplaced letters, overheard words, or introductions made in poor judgment—mistakes that were usually limited in scope and could often be contained. Today, that world is gone. Privacy no longer lives in archives; it lives—or vanishes—inside digital systems.

Every login, transaction, email, or card swipe leaves behind a trace. To the casual user, invisible. To regulators, investigators, or competitors, these traces form a map of behavior and influence. What once remained hidden by default must now be hidden by design.

Silent Power cannot rely only on legal frameworks or on lifestyle restraint. In the twenty-first century, it must be engineered into the digital layer itself. To live discreetly now means deciding what is recorded, what can be linked, and what is inferred. It means building habits and infrastructures where devices, networks, and communications protect sovereignty instead of surrendering it.

Digital silence does not mean disconnection. It means using technology without being consumed by it. Common advice—download a

VPN, avoid public Wi-Fi, switch to encrypted messaging—scratches the surface. Tools alone do not make architecture. What follows is deeper: the structural foundations of cyber discretion. We will see how sophisticated actors design invisible infrastructures, separate roles across digital identities, control metadata as carefully as capital, and preserve sovereignty in a world designed to extract data.

This is not paranoia. It is configuration—digital sovereignty as the natural extension of Silent Power. Without it, even the best legal structures collapse under the weight of an environment where data never sleeps.

What Actually Exposes You Online

Most people believe their privacy is intact if their passwords are strong, their social media settings are locked down, and their chats are encrypted. That belief is misplaced. The real danger rarely comes from hacks or breaches. It comes from structure: using the wrong tool in the wrong context, mixing personal and professional roles on the same device, leaving metadata embedded in documents or images, or relying on default settings designed for convenience, not discretion.

Silent operators are not betrayed by a single message. They are betrayed by patterns. What compromises them is not what they say but how the system records that they said it, when, and through which channel.

The Myth of Content Security

Much of the digital-security world obsesses over content—encrypting files, securing chats, protecting documents. Encryption matters, but it is not the heart of the issue. Metadata is.

Metadata is the invisible but permanent record that sits behind every interaction: who you contacted, when, from where, on what device, through which service, and how often. Unlike content, metadata is routinely stored, indexed, and shared. Encryption hides the words. Metadata reveals the structure of your life.

Worse still, metadata is legally accessible. Frameworks like the U.S. CLOUD Act or the network of Mutual Legal Assistance Treaties allow states to share this information across borders, often with minimal notice to the user.

The strategist must therefore accept one rule: metadata is permanent. Every login, message, or connection feeds into a fingerprint that can be reconstructed and, if necessary, weaponized. Silence online is not the absence of speech—it is the active management of what systems can infer.

Platforms That Incriminate Without Warning

Most compromises of digital discretion come not from breaches but from the platforms people use daily. Convenience is the lure; traceability is the price.

Google's Gmail, Docs, and Calendar appear as separate tools, yet they feed a single data spine where every keystroke is cross-referenced. Microsoft's Outlook, OneDrive, and Teams work the same way, synchronizing activity across personal and corporate devices by default. Dropbox and iCloud eliminate boundaries altogether, storing drafts and images in environments where deletion is rarely final. Meta's WhatsApp and Instagram weave messaging, contacts, and geolocation into one integrated identity profile.

Individually, these platforms are secure for casual use. Structurally, they are dangerous when discretion is paramount. A confidential legal note sent through Gmail while logged into a personal Google account does not just transmit words—it anchors the relationship into a wider ecosystem of search history, location data, and device fingerprints.

The principle is simple: tools must fit intent. Platforms designed for frictionless connection are not built for boundaries. Their purpose is to integrate, not to protect. What serves the public well is often fatal for the discreet.

Exposure Through Devices, Not Decisions

Even the most disciplined strategist can be betrayed by their devices. Phones, laptops, tablets, watches, and even connected cars are not neutral—they are designed to sync, log, and transmit continuously. What appears private is usually a channel feeding remote servers and data brokers.

Exposure rarely comes through spectacular breaches. It seeps through subtle leaks: Bluetooth beacons mapping proximity, SIM cards anchoring identity across borders, default cloud syncs moving files to foreign servers, predictive text revealing usage patterns.

The risk multiplies at borders. Under routine "inspections," states may copy entire devices. In places such as the United States, China, or under the Five Eyes alliance, this is done without notice or warrant. The user often never knows.

For the strategist, the first principle is non-negotiable: no device is truly private. Devices are not archives of thought—they are surfaces visible to others. They must be treated as temporary instruments: compartmentalized, replaceable, and used only with clear purpose. A phone is not a lifelong companion. A laptop is not a vault. Even conveniences such as smart cars or voice assistants are not helpers; they are sensors that must be managed or excluded.

Silent Power in the digital age begins not with what you say, but with what you carry—and how you carry it. To confuse a device with privacy is to surrender sovereignty. To treat it as a bounded tool is the first step in reclaiming it.

Behavioral Leakage: The Invisible Exposure

In the digital age, exposure often has little to do with what you say or publish. You can stay silent on social media, avoid emails tied to your real name, and operate through pseudonyms across multiple platforms—yet still be identified with surprising precision. The culprit is behavioral leakage: the trail created not by content, but by the way you interact with machines.

Modern algorithms track more than words. They analyze how quickly you type, the cadence of your keystrokes, how your mouse moves, the rhythm of your scrolling, and even the pauses before you click. These seemingly trivial details form a behavioral fingerprint—unique, consistent, and extremely hard to disguise. This "digital exhaust" becomes a secondary identity, one that confirms who you are no matter what name you use.

When combined with cookies, device IDs, and browser signatures, behavioral leakage makes anonymity fragile. Advertisers, governments, and technology platforms use these signals to connect activity across pseudonyms, VPNs, and even burner devices. The illusion of separation collapses because the system doesn't need your name; it only needs the rhythm of your behavior.

Many assume that opening a new email account or adopting a pseudonym creates distance. In reality, unless those accounts are used on separate devices, networks, and routines, they are linked almost instantly. Your login hours, hesitation patterns, and navigation style betray you more than any username ever could.

Silent Power requires more than technical hygiene. It demands behavioral discipline. It is not enough to control what you say or which tool you use. Your cadence online must itself be unreadable. To succeed, the strategist learns not only to build clean systems, but to live inside them consistently, refusing to let unconscious patterns undo carefully designed architectures.

Invisibility is not simply about concealing information. It is about neutralizing the signatures that algorithms rely on to assemble fragments into a complete profile. Silence, therefore, extends beyond speech. It must be embedded in behavior.

Corporate Infrastructure and Email Traceability

A structure may look flawless on paper yet fail in practice because of something as ordinary as an email. Silent operators often underestimate how much exposure comes not from their legal arrangements or lifestyle choices, but from poorly configured digital infrastructure. One mismanaged server, a casual choice of registrar, or an overlooked email header can undo years of strategic design.

Every email contains an invisible architecture of metadata: domains, relays, IP addresses, timestamps. Even when the content is encrypted, these headers expose who communicated, when, and through which system. If tied to a personal domain or consolidated into one corporate identity, they create connections that no strategist can afford.

Domain names themselves carry risk. A company may be structured offshore with impeccable care, yet its domain is registered in a high-surveillance jurisdiction, exposing ownership through WHOIS records or registrar subpoenas. Cloud-based services add another layer of vulnerability by duplicating correspondence on foreign servers, making them accessible through court orders or intelligence-sharing agreements.

The discreet strategist treats digital infrastructure as part of the architecture of power. Domains are registered through trustees or neutral entities in protective jurisdictions. Email systems are compartmentalized: personal, corporate, and fiduciary roles are separated across distinct infrastructures. Communication flows through secure environments where metadata is minimized, anonymized, or fragmented by design.

This is not technical paranoia–it is operational logic. Just as a poorly drafted shareholder agreement can weaken a company, a careless email setup can expose entire networks. In Silent Power, digital infrastructure is managed with the same rigor as law or finance. A message is never just a message. It is also a signal, a fingerprint, and, if mishandled, a liability.

Domain Names and WHOIS Exposure

Every enterprise—whether a company, a foundation, or a discreet advisory service—requires a domain name. Yet this small detail often becomes the weakest point in an otherwise refined structure. Too many register domains under personal names or traceable entities, leaving a trail of data that undermines years of careful planning.

A WHOIS entry is never just technical. It can reveal registrant names, addresses, administrative contacts, registrar details, and the jurisdiction of registration. Even creation dates and renewal cycles can be cross-referenced with DNS history to expose links across projects or to reconstruct timelines. Months of work dispersing assets across jurisdictions can collapse through a single careless registration.

Registrar "privacy shields" provide only partial protection. Historical DNS archives, subpoenas, and forensic tools often pierce these layers. Worse still, many privacy services are owned by the same registrars, placing data under the same subpoena regimes as direct ownership. The anonymity they offer is cosmetic at best.

Strategic configuration requires more than toggling a privacy option. Domains should be registered through trustee layers or nominee entities, never in the strategist's name. Jurisdictional dispersion adds further protection: a registrar in Iceland, administrative contacts in Panama, servers in Switzerland. This fragmentation ensures no single provider or authority sees the entire picture. Administrative emails must exist solely for domain management, never linked to personal or operational accounts. Content systems like WordPress must remain decoupled from the legal entity behind the brand.

A domain is not a casual purchase. It is a structural declaration of jurisdiction, control, and ownership. If it points back—through name, entity, or IP—it ceases to be neutral and becomes a liability.

In Silent Power, even the smallest surface is fortified. A domain is not merely an address; it is part of the defensive wall. To treat it otherwise is to let a gate open in an otherwise silent fortress.

Email Systems: Traceability, Metadata, and Correlation Risk

Email remains one of the riskiest tools in any digital setup—not because of the words it carries, but because of the architecture it discloses. Every message is a bundle of signals. Alongside its visible content, it transmits identifiers: the originating IP address, the device signature, the time zone, the default language, and a full header trail mapping its path across the internet.

Modern protocols add further exposure. Standards like SPF, DKIM, and DMARC confirm legitimacy, but they also tie the message back to the sender's domain or platform. Hidden headers disclose which software was used, how the message traveled, and whether it was opened or tracked. A single email can betray who you are, where you were, and how your system operates—even if the body of the message is encrypted.

Mainstream providers amplify these risks. Gmail, Outlook, and their equivalents are not neutral utilities; they are integral parts of profiling ecosystems. Google unifies Gmail with Maps, YouTube, Calendar, and Drive into a single behavioral profile. Microsoft does the same with Outlook, Office 365, OneDrive, and Teams. Messages are indexed, scanned, and stored indefinitely. An email is never just a communication—it is evidence feeding a permanent identity model.

Alternatives exist. Services such as ProtonMail in Switzerland, Tutanota in Germany, or Mailfence in Belgium operate under stronger jurisdictional safeguards and open cryptographic standards. For those with resources, self-hosted servers offer maximum autonomy—provided they are supported by hardened infrastructure and the expertise to maintain them. Yet no platform is secure if used carelessly. A discreet address loses its value the moment it is linked to a recipient's mainstream inbox, or when it is accessed through a traceable device or network. Forgotten metadata in attachments, reply chains, or timestamps can undo years of careful architecture.

Mitigation is about strategy, not gadgets. Each entity, role, or project must use its own dedicated email identity, with no overlap. Tracking pixels, autoresponders, and signatures must be disabled. Sensitive communication should run through aliases or proxy domains, preventing external observers from tracing activities to a single core address. Personal correspondence must never overlap with operational work, and archives must be encrypted, tightly controlled, and purged on schedule.

An email address is never just a convenience. It is a locator, a beacon that maps relationships, jurisdictions, and vulnerabilities. Managed without discipline, it betrays the very system it was built to protect. Handled correctly, it becomes invisible—functional, but unreadable to those trying to decode it.

Cloud Platforms and Collateral Traceability

Beyond email and domains, the greatest risk often lies in everyday collaboration tools. Services like Google Docs, Microsoft Teams, Dropbox, Slack, Notion, Trello, Asana, Adobe Creative Cloud,

Figma, or Canva promise efficiency and global access. Yet they are built for traceability. Every action leaves a record: user IDs, timestamps, version histories, and usage patterns. Together, these logs create maps of who worked with whom, when, and from where.

The danger grows when collaborators lack the same discipline. Picture this: you operate under a carefully designed alias, using encrypted communication and compartmentalized infrastructure. A partner, unaware of your protocols, saves a draft with your alias in the filename and uploads it to their personal Google Drive. That file then syncs across devices, cloud backups, and accounts. If their system is later compromised—through a breach, litigation subpoena, or simple negligence—your identity is now embedded in evidence you never touched.

Discretion, then, cannot depend on your practices alone. It must be institutionalized. Projects and entities must each use distinct platforms, with no mixing of personal and professional tools. Contracts should include confidentiality clauses that govern storage, sharing, and deletion protocols. Sensitive material should never sit on mainstream collaboration platforms unless neutralized, either by encryption on zero-knowledge systems or with watermarks that trace leaks back to their source.

Discipline extends to exits as well. When a collaborator departs—whether an employee, a partner, or a vendor—formal off-boarding is non-negotiable: revoke access, erase data, dismantle shared accounts, and contain liability. Silent systems fail less because of their architects than because of weak links left unchecked.

True discretion is never personal. It is systemic. It resides in workflows, in the behavior of collaborators, and in the enforcement of boundaries. Only when privacy is embedded across the entire chain does it become resilient enough to survive.

Aligning Infrastructure with Jurisdictional Logic

Even the most refined structure—a trust, a foundation, a holding network—can be undermined if its digital infrastructure is anchored in the wrong jurisdiction. Encryption is vital, but it is not sufficient. Exposure is ultimately determined by where data is stored and which legal system governs it.

In the United States, the CLOUD Act, secret FISA orders, and the intelligence-sharing framework of the Five Eyes alliance allow authorities to demand data from service providers without user knowledge. In the European Union, transparency directives and anti-money-laundering frameworks impose disclosure obligations that may run against the privacy design of offshore systems. Even in stable jurisdictions, bilateral treaties and MLATs allow data to flow across borders with little resistance.

For the silent strategist, the rule is clear: hosting is never neutral. The jurisdiction of your servers, your clouds, and your backups dictates which authorities can reach them, under what terms, and with what level of discretion. A Liechtenstein foundation managing Swiss assets loses coherence if its documents are stored on U.S. servers. A Dubai-based family office is weakened if its governance archives sit in the EU. An offshore holding in Nevis becomes vulnerable if its digital backbone rests in Canada.

Strategic alignment requires coherence. Assets governed in Switzerland belong in Swiss data centers. Structures domiciled in Liechtenstein must rely on neutral European providers. Entities based in Singapore or Dubai must select local or allied jurisdictions that uphold the same principles of discretion. Every piece of infrastructure must reflect the same design logic, so that adversaries find no contradictions to exploit.

Discretion does not mean avoiding law. It means choosing which law governs your footprint. The strategist does not allow chance to decide where their data resides. They select deliberately, ensuring that hosting, storage, and communication systems are aligned with structural intent. In Silent Power, every layer—from statutes to servers—exists to defend sovereignty.

Digital Tools for Secure Operations

Building a discreet digital infrastructure is not only about avoiding exposure. It is about actively shaping a set of tools that can sustain operations without eroding sovereignty. For those managing cross-border influence, complex structures, or sensitive assets, the selection of digital tools is as strategic as choosing a jurisdiction or a fiduciary.

The challenge is that many tools sold as "secure" or "private" do not deliver what they promise. Some are little more than privacy theater—wrapped in the language of encryption while quietly harvesting metadata or routing traffic through compromised jurisdictions. At the other end are platforms so technical, unstable, or poorly supported that they collapse in practice. Neither extreme works for someone operating under Silent Power.

What is required is a carefully balanced set of instruments that combine four qualities:

- Security: strong cryptography with minimal metadata leakage.
- Jurisdictional alignment: providers rooted in countries that reinforce, rather than undermine, the legal structure around them.
- Usability: tools that can be deployed in daily life without constant breakdowns or endless workarounds.
- Control: systems that allow the user to dictate access, continuity, and compartmentalization instead of trusting corporate promises.

When these conditions converge, technology becomes part of the strategy rather than a point of weakness.

The discreet strategist assembles an ecosystem that is layered, redundant, and segmented. Communications platforms are chosen not for fashion but for their jurisdictional logic. Cloud services are vetted for sovereignty rather than convenience. Browsers, password managers, and document systems are compartmentalized, each assigned to a defined role so that no single environment ever holds the full picture.

The goal is not to live offline or shun modern systems. It is to build a digital environment that supports influence, mobility, and decision-making without leaving signatures that can later be weaponized.

In the following sections, we examine the categories of tools that matter most: encrypted communications, secure storage, anonymized browsing, metadata management, and layered authentication. Each must be selected and configured deliberately so that privacy is not an afterthought but an operating principle.

Communication Tools: Messaging Without Trace

Encrypted messaging has become mainstream, yet most platforms fall short of the rigor required for genuine discretion. End-to-end encryption by itself is not enough. What matters is metadata, jurisdiction, and operational discipline.

A few options stand out. Signal remains the most transparent: open-source, independently audited, and committed to retaining virtually no metadata. Its disappearing messages and secure channels are suited to time-sensitive exchanges. Session goes further, removing the need for phone numbers and routing communication through a decentralized network, making it well adapted to burner devices and unattributable contacts. Threema, based in Switzerland, benefits from strong encryption and a jurisdiction where privacy has institutional weight. It avoids the phone number trap entirely. Silent Phone, developed for diplomats and executives, integrates encrypted voice and messaging into enterprise-grade protocols.

But tools are only as strong as the discipline behind them. Secure platforms turn into liabilities if used casually. Communication must remain device-specific, never synced across clouds that leave redundant copies. Features such as contact syncing, read receipts, typing indicators, and automated backups are best disabled. Personal channels must never overlap with operational ones, and sensitive networks must remain in their own silos.

Equally important is what not to use. WhatsApp and Telegram, despite partial encryption, fail under scrutiny. Their ownership structures, data retention practices, and integration into surveillance ecosystems make them incompatible with sensitive operations. They are designed for reach, not discretion.

For the silent strategist, privacy is not defined by the content of a message but by the system that delivers it and the traces that remain afterward. The aim is communication that functions seamlessly yet leaves nothing meaningful behind.

Secure Browsing and Access: Where and How You Connect

Browsers and internet connections are constant vectors of exposure. Even without logging into accounts, each session leaks information: browser fingerprint, IP address, DNS queries, and traffic behavior. A VPN alone, if poorly configured, often leaves gaps large enough to map your movements across jurisdictions.

Discreet browsing requires intentional design. Hardened versions of Brave or Firefox can disable telemetry, obscure fingerprints, and isolate sessions. Tor Browser provides anonymity but is too slow and conspicuous for routine use. VPNs should never come from mainstream providers rooted in surveillance-heavy countries. Instead, the discreet operator uses private VPN instances—OpenVPN or WireGuard—hosted on offshore servers in privacy-protective jurisdictions such as Iceland, Switzerland, or Seychelles.

DNS queries are another weak point. Services like NextDNS or DNS0.eu reduce leaks and provide filtering capacity. At the hardware level, tools like pfSense or Firewalla segment networks and block devices that attempt to "phone home" without consent.

Yet infrastructure alone is not enough. Discipline matters just as much. Sensitive accounts should never be accessed from hotel Wi-Fi or public hotspots. Distinct legal roles–director, investor, advisor–must operate in separate browser identities. Caches must be cleared regularly, and outbound traffic monitored, since idle applications often broadcast signals without consent.

Access, in this context, is not only technical. It is legal. Where you connect from determines not just speed but jurisdiction, obligation, and vulnerability. In Silent Power, browsing is never casual–it is sovereign by design.

File Management and Document Security

Silent operators handle documents that are more than records. Trust deeds, shareholder agreements, internal mandates, and asset registers form the skeleton of influence itself. These files are not only vulnerable to hackers–they are equally exposed to subpoenas, regulatory capture, and careless disclosure. Protecting them requires more than passwords or folders. It demands a file system that mirrors the architecture of discretion.

Several tools provide the necessary foundation. **Tresorit,** headquartered in Switzerland, offers end-to-end encryption and strong jurisdictional protection outside U.S. surveillance regimes. **Sync.com** in Canada provides zero-knowledge storage with private encryption keys. For those who must work within mainstream platforms, **Cryptomator** creates local encrypted vaults that can sync even with Dropbox or Google

Drive, though these services remain structurally misaligned with discreet operations. **VeraCrypt** delivers full-disk encryption with hidden containers, offering plausible deniability in case of coercion. For complete control, self-hosted environments–such as **OnlyOffice** integrated with **Nextcloud**–allow collaboration and secure storage under the strategist's chosen jurisdiction.

Yet tools are effective only when paired with discipline. Silent operators watermark sensitive files to trace leaks and compartmentalize rigorously so that corporate, family, and client records never coexist in the same vault. Multiple encrypted containers are maintained: some functional, others decoys. Backups are never kept locally or within the same legal reach. Instead, they are placed offshore, stored under sovereign conditions that reduce exposure.

The system itself communicates the strategy. Silence is not about encrypting everything. It is about encrypting the essential and placing it where no one is looking. A discreet architecture is only as strong as the discipline with which documents are designed and stored.

Passwords, Access, and Digital Succession

The strongest structures often collapse from within–not through outside attack, but because of lost credentials, weak recovery habits, or accidental disclosure. The most common vulnerability is not the adversary. It is the lapse of discipline.

Proper access begins with encrypted credential management. **Bitwarden** and **KeePassXC** offer secure vaults with options for self-hosting or private cloud storage. Hardware keys such as **YubiKey** or **Nitrokey** add physical barriers against phishing and unauthorized logins, particularly for email and server access. Highly sensitive protocols can be stored in encrypted USB drives, duplicated, and deposited in separate secure jurisdictions. For long-term continuity, sealed recovery kits should be printed and stored in multiple locations, protecting against both accident and political instability.

Governance is as critical as technology. Even within family structures, role-based access must prevail. Credentials should only be released through predefined protocols—sealed succession letters, notarized mandates, or escrow agreements with fiduciaries. Remote revocation and time-delayed controls should be embedded wherever possible, allowing strategists to rescind access if compromise occurs.

In Silent Power, continuity outlives the strategist. Digital succession is not paranoia—it is survival by design. A structure endures only if its keys remain in the right hands and never fall into the wrong ones.

Designing Multi-Layered Cyber Discretion

Silent Power never rests on a single app, password, or clever trick. It emerges from architecture—a layered design where every element of the digital system plays a defined role, remains separated from others, and collectively reduces exposure.

Layering does not mean piling up software. It means segmenting identities, roles, and data flows across different providers, jurisdictions, and devices so that no single compromise reveals the whole. One device is used for travel, another for negotiations, another for family matters. Storage is split across multiple providers under distinct legal frameworks. Communication is divided: some channels for casual traffic, some for operational directives, a few for sensitive exchanges that must leave no trail.

This is not complexity for show. It is resilience by structure. Just as no single corporate registry should reveal the full scope of a family's wealth, no single server should reveal the full scope of a strategist's life.

Law and technology must mirror one another. Legal discretion collapses if digital systems betray it, and digital discretion is worthless if legal structures do not reinforce it. Silent Power thrives only when both dimensions align into a coherent architecture of silence.

Segregation of Roles and Identities

Each role—founder, advisor, investor, board member, or philanthropist—carries a distinct risk profile. Combining them within one account, device, or browser creates cross-contamination. A subpoena aimed at a board position can expose family archives. An audit focused on one entity can unravel another. The problem is not misconduct—it is correlation.

The solution is operational segregation. Each role must have its own environment: separate devices, separate browser identities, separate accounts. Aliases and routing layers prevent direct links. Usernames, passwords, and recovery mechanisms are never repeated across functions.

Strategic infrastructure remains clean only if roles remain divided. Personal accounts never touch professional systems. Sensitive communications never travel through casual platforms. Once systems entangle, exposures entangle—and narrative control is lost.

This is not paranoia. It is protocol. Because lawful activity, misread or aggregated in the wrong context, can still be weaponized. The strategist does not seek disappearance. They seek undecodability: present in outcome, unreadable in form.

Layered Jurisdictional Mapping

Digital discretion collapses when hosted in the wrong jurisdiction. Encryption matters, but where data resides matters more.

In the United States, the **CLOUD Act** and secret FISA orders allow access to servers without notifying the user. In the European Union, transparency and anti-money laundering directives compel disclosures that may conflict with offshore privacy structures. Even stable jurisdictions rely on mutual assistance treaties that open backdoors for foreign authorities.

For the silent strategist, hosting is never neutral. Email may be placed in Switzerland, domains registered through Iceland or Seychelles, documents stored in encrypted form in Liechtenstein, and VPNs routed through Finland or Panama. Each layer is chosen for its legal shield, not convenience.

The goal is not fragmentation for its own sake. It is resilience. If one authority gains access to communications, they still lack storage. If one server is compromised, the rest remain sealed. No single entry point reveals the entire system. Jurisdiction here is more than geography–it is a firewall woven into design.

Operational Compartmentalization

Most leaks come not from hackers but from within: an assistant syncing files into the wrong folder, a collaborator reusing credentials, or a vendor mixing systems. Exposure is rarely forced. It is usually accidental.

The countermeasure is compartmentalization. Each project, entity, or mandate must operate in its own sealed environment. Access must be role-based: directors see what directors need, contractors see only what their work requires. Even internal staff should face context-based authentication, so no one role unlocks the whole system.

The most powerful rule: no individual, not even the strategist, should hold universal access in one place. Authority must be distributed, revocable, and replaceable.

Resilience is not having every key. It is ensuring that no single map exists to the entire architecture.

Silent Audits and Digital Simulations

Design alone is never enough. Just as financial or legal frameworks must be stress-tested, digital discretion cannot be assumed. A system that appears robust on paper may unravel the moment it is pressed under real conditions. Silent systems demand active pressure to expose weak points—through simulations, penetration testing, or adversarial modeling.

Audits must examine what most overlook: metadata hidden in PDF files, headers embedded in emails, or location data buried in photos. Devices must be scanned for silent activity from microphones, cameras, or tracking services. Behavioral overlaps—usernames reused across contexts, cookies that bridge browsing sessions, contact lists that betray compartments—can quietly undo entire architectures. Forensic traffic analysis can be even more damaging, allowing observers to map flows of activity without ever reading content. The decisive question is simple: if one device or account were breached, would it lead straight to the core—or only to ambiguity?

These exercises cannot be delegated to IT alone. They must be reviewed from legal, reputational, and strategic angles. For digital silence, the goal is not to erase every trace. It is to ensure that whatever remains leads nowhere significant.

The Role of Continuous Cyber Discipline

Discretion is not a static configuration. It is a living practice. The most carefully layered architecture can become obsolete within weeks if vigilance falters.

Every update carries risk. Platforms shift their policies without notice. Jurisdictions expand surveillance treaties. Devices reconnect or synchronize by default. What was discreet yesterday may already be archived today. In a digital world, silence erodes unless it is renewed.

Silent Power is sustained not by perfection but by rhythm—consistent review of data flows, regular verification of providers' jurisdictions, timely replacement of tools that lose integrity. It is less about building the ultimate firewall than about cultivating habits of inspection and adaptation.

Discretion, in this sense, is awareness. It is the discipline of questioning before acting, resisting convenience when it conflicts with structure, and treating every system as temporary. The greatest exposure is not technical. It is psychological—the belief that what was private once remains private still. Silent Power rejects that illusion. It assumes volatility and builds rituals of inspection, rotation, and renewal.

Discretion as a Daily Practice

Most failures arise not from flawed tools but from human slips. A single act—logging into a strategic account on a personal phone, accepting an invite through a private calendar, forwarding files with unclean metadata, or posting online from an IP tied to confidential operations—can compromise an otherwise flawless design.

Cyber discretion must be practiced daily. Before sending a file, confirm that it is clean and the recipient appropriate. Before logging in, consider the device, the jurisdiction, and the context. Before connecting, verify that the browser and VPN match the role. Before storing information, check whether the chosen location creates legal or reputational exposure. And before writing, ask whether the words could withstand disclosure.

The strategist lives as if every system were monitored, not out of paranoia, but by design. Resilience is not optimism. It is the outcome of repeated caution.

The Cost of Inconsistency

The most dangerous breach is not the spectacular hack but the subtle contradiction. Inconsistency makes systems legible.

A strategist may build around ProtonMail, only to reply once through Gmail. They may separate devices meticulously, then reveal location data through an unsecured Zoom session. VPNs chosen for speed rather than jurisdictional logic betray their own architecture. A casual LinkedIn post linked to a discreet identity can provide the missing puzzle piece to investigators.

These small deviations enable triangulation, allowing adversaries to connect fragments into a coherent picture. Once mapped, the structure loses its protective ambiguity. The silent strategist knows that the true failure is rarely catastrophic. It is the inconsistency that exposes the whole.

Training and Alignment of Close Collaborators

A system is only as discreet as its weakest participant. Assistants, collaborators, family members, or vendors can undo years of design through misunderstanding. Silent architecture cannot rely on intuition. It requires training and codified rules.

Core principles must be explicit: no mixing of roles on a single device or inbox, no forwarding without metadata scrubbing, no reuse of credentials, no assumption that cloud backups are invisible, and no operational discussion over consumer platforms like WhatsApp or Messenger. Protocols must be written, rehearsed, and tested with scenarios: *What if this account is compromised? What if this device is seized?*

Legacy families increasingly train heirs in cyber discretion, ensuring they understand not only tools but logic—the discipline to operate without leaving footprints. This is not IT support. It is continuity planning. In Silent Power, hygiene is not optional. It is intergenerational strategy.

Updating the Architecture: Strategic Maintenance

No system remains discreet by default. Technologies age, providers shift policy, jurisdictions realign. Stability itself becomes a risk.

Maintenance requires rhythm. Core platforms—email, storage, VPNs, devices—should be reviewed quarterly. Jurisdictional maps revised annually. Collaborators updated every six months. Emergency rehearsals conducted regularly: *What if you were hacked, subpoenaed, or forced to exit a jurisdiction within 48 hours?* New tools must be tested before older ones fail.

This is not paranoia. It is governance. Your digital presence is your territory, and like any territory, it must be audited, defended, and maintained. Silent Power is not passive. It is stewardship.

Final Note - Digital Discretion Is a Living System

Digital discretion is not secrecy. It is design. And design must evolve.

To master Silent Power in the digital era is to stop viewing privacy as a product—a secure app, a private server, or a new device. Privacy is an ecosystem: the interplay of systems, behaviors, jurisdictions, and collaborators. Each layer reinforces the others, and each must adapt as conditions change.

The digital environment is built for visibility. To remain discreet is to resist that design with one of your own. Visibility is cheap. Discretion is costly. But its returns are freedom, leverage, and peace in a world that never stops watching.

Silent Power does not rely on secrecy. It relies on architecture. And architecture, when maintained as a living system, becomes the shield that makes influence possible without exposure.

CHAPTER VI - Legal Visibility vs Real Exposure

Modern compliance systems are built on the premise that visibility equals accountability. Governments, tax agencies, and supervisory bodies have developed increasingly aggressive tools to determine who owns what, where, and why. Yet despite this drive toward transparency, regulatory sightlines remain partial, delayed, and highly dependent on context.

For the strategist, understanding what regulators truly see—and what they only assume—is essential. It allows for structures that are fully compliant, but still layered, resilient, and resistant to easy mapping.

Layers of Legal Visibility: Shareholders, UBOs, and Functional Roles

Legal visibility operates in tiers. At the surface are the formal owners: names recorded in shareholder lists, land registries, or membership logs. A step deeper lies the category of ultimate beneficial ownership (UBO)—the individuals who control or profit from an entity, often defined by thresholds such as 25 percent equity or voting power. Beyond that are the functional roles: directors, managers, signatories, and other representatives whose names appear in filings or mandates.

Most jurisdictions now impose some version of UBO disclosure under global standards like AML directives, CRS, FATCA, or OECD rules. But this visibility is not absolute. Thresholds shape what must be declared: a 24.9 percent shareholding, for example, may fall below the trigger point. Legal form matters too, since trusts, foundations, and partnerships are treated differently across systems, sometimes with greater opacity. Jurisdiction is decisive: a trust declared in the United Kingdom may remain undisclosed in Liechtenstein. Nominee directors or fiduciaries add yet another layer, separating legal appearance from practical control.

The key point is that regulators monitor formal connections, not operational logic—unless filings contradict each other or gaps are left open. When structures are designed with consistency, legal visibility is not denied but distributed, diluted, and made non-threatening.

Jurisdictional Asymmetry in Disclosure Requirements

There is no uniform global rulebook. Each jurisdiction sets its own disclosure thresholds, formats, and reporting cycles. This asymmetry creates structural gaps the strategist can navigate. Visibility becomes a matter of *where*, *when*, and *how* disclosure is required—not whether it exists at all.

Switzerland requires UBO declarations for banking relationships, but has no centralized public register. Delaware LLCs need not reveal shareholders or directors. Liechtenstein protects the privacy of foundation beneficiaries unless compelled by court order. The United Arab Emirates allows full corporate ownership with no public officer or shareholder registers.

Even where transparency is emphasized, systems remain fragmented. A UBO declaration filed with a tax authority may not cross-check against land ownership. Commercial registries often remain unlinked to banking disclosures or trust records. This disconnection allows for separation: ownership in one country, management in another, and benefit in a third—each shielded by its own legal environment.

The global system is not integrated. It is a patchwork. And it is within that patchwork that discretion is built.

Delayed vs. Real-Time Reporting: The Window of Control

One of the strategist's least recognized advantages is time. Visibility is rarely instantaneous. Annual filings, periodic declarations, and delayed information exchanges create natural buffers—windows in which adjustments can be made before records catch up.

Corporate filings may be required only once a year, leaving months between a change in reality and its formal inscription. Beneficial ownership declarations are often triggered only when thresholds are crossed. CRS and FATCA operate on yearly cycles, and the data exchanged is frequently partial or outdated.

These gaps can be used strategically. A position can be exited just before establishing tax nexus. Voting rights can be reshaped ahead of an audit. Nominees can be replaced before registries update. Management functions can be shifted outside reporting windows.

Visibility is episodic, not continuous. And in most systems, a fact must be declared repeatedly before it becomes consistently visible.

Legal Obligations vs. Investigatory Access

Disclosure is not exposure. To declare something to an authority does not mean that it is open to all eyes. The law distinguishes between regulatory obligations, investigatory access, and public availability. Silent architecture thrives within these distinctions.

Regulatory obligations require information to be filed with competent authorities, but access is typically limited to justified requests.

Public access is rare and often confined to specific registries. For example, a beneficial owner may be declared to a tax agency yet remain absent from corporate registers. A trust deed may be lodged with a notary but remain sealed unless a court compels disclosure. An operating agreement may define governance internally without ever entering the public record.

What matters is not only what is declared, but who can see it, under which conditions, and at what point in time.

- Regulators may access data, but only after a formal request.
- Banks see what clients disclose—and here, narrative management becomes decisive.
- Courts can compel production, but only under the correct jurisdiction and procedure.
- Journalists and private actors are confined to public databases, not to internal mandates or fiduciary agreements.

The strategist works on the assumption that all information may eventually surface, but also designs so that its emergence is delayed, fragmented, or rendered strategically irrelevant.

Strategic Use of Public Registers

Public registers are often seen as the sworn enemies of discretion. They exist to collect names, titles, and formal connections, feeding the machinery of compliance, taxation, and surveillance. At first glance, their presence appears to erase the very possibility of privacy. But this view is incomplete. For a strategist, registers are not only constraints to be endured; they can be repurposed into shields—interfaces that fulfill legal obligations while concealing the true design of control.

A public record is never the full story. It is a fragment, a formal snapshot meant to serve regulators, courts, or parties seeking certainty. To mistake this surface for the essence of governance is a fundamental error. The listing of a director in a company registry, the entry of a shareholder with a token percentage, or the filing of a trust deed in accordance with local requirements does not reveal who sets strategy, who defines purpose, or who ultimately directs outcomes. It reveals only what the law requires at that level of formality.

The strategist therefore approaches registers with deliberate precision. The goal is not to refuse disclosure, but to sculpt it. Nominee directors, fiduciary shareholders, or corporate vehicles may appear in the registry, while real authority remains in private agreements, confidential mandates, or internal protocols. A holding company may be registered in a transparent jurisdiction, but its control may rest elsewhere—in a foundation, trust, or fiduciary contract shielded from external mapping.

When properly designed, the visible layer becomes a compliant shell: accurate, minimal, legally valid, yet never a faithful map of the underlying system. Rather than a threat, the registry becomes a buffer—a surface that absorbs scrutiny while the real engine of governance operates silently behind it.

What Public Records Reveal—and What They Don't

Registers vary widely across jurisdictions in both content and accessibility. At minimum, they provide incorporation data: entity name, legal form, registration number, and date of creation. Some disclose directors, managers, or shareholders, whether in full, partially, or only above certain thresholds. Others may list articles of association, registered addresses, auditors, or declared sectors of activity. In rare instances, registers include UBO data or annual accounts.

Yet the omissions are more telling than the inclusions. Private mandates, voting pacts, side agreements, and beneficial use clauses are never filed. Letters of wishes, protector appointments, and succession instructions remain confidential. The logic of governance—who gives orders, how decisions are shaped, and where influence actually resides—does not appear.

Even when records are accessible, their interpretation remains narrow. A shareholder may have no real authority. A director may act under binding fiduciary instruction. An entity listed as owner may lack enjoyment or effective control of the underlying asset.

Registers display form, not substance. What governs is what lies outside them: the unregistered, the unrecorded, the deliberately insulated.

Using Buffer Roles, Nominee Appointments, and Visible Fronts

One of the most refined strategies in dealing with registers is the calculated deployment of roles that are visible but lack true authority. This is not deception—it is structural design, separating compliance from command.

Nominee directors may sit on boards and appear in filings, yet their authority is defined and limited elsewhere. Corporate shareholders may hold equity on behalf of beneficial owners, acting as formal intermediaries. Administrative managers may sign off on filings without influencing strategy. Advisory boards may be listed for signaling purposes but carry no operational weight.

Each role is intentional. They satisfy formal requirements, convey legitimacy—sometimes even prestige, when a respected fiduciary or law firm is placed in the foreground—and redirect attention away from the strategist. Visibility is managed, never improvised. Every name that appears is placed with care.

Managing Substance Declarations and Formal Responsibilities

In high-compliance jurisdictions, regulators demand more than titles. They look for substance: evidence that an entity is active where it claims to be. This may involve board meetings within the jurisdiction, tax registrations, invoicing, and other operational markers.

Meeting these demands does not require surrendering discretion. Directors can be appointed with narrow, revocable mandates. Local meetings can be convened without exposing the true strategist, as long as formalities are followed. Administrative duties can be outsourced to licensed providers whose role is functional, not strategic. Board resolutions can be drafted to satisfy compliance requirements while preserving strategic flexibility in practice.

When integrated properly, substance becomes not an obstacle but a design element—proof of legal validity that coexists with structural separation. What is visible fulfills the law. What is decisive remains outside the orbit of routine oversight.

How to Comply Without Exposing Command

The last layer of strategic design lies in building a public surface that satisfies every legal duty yet reveals nothing essential. This surface is not about concealment, but curation. It presents information that is accurate, complete, and at the same time strategically neutral.

A registry may list directors who hold no ownership or voting power. Jurisdictions are selected because their laws limit public access, as in Switzerland, Liechtenstein, the UAE, or Nevis. Entities may publish reports, file accounts, and appear compliant, while real authority remains anchored in private agreements.

Fiduciaries or corporate vehicles can be placed in view, absorbing attention while the deeper layers stay protected—for example, a Swiss SA or German GmbH owned by a foundation whose beneficiaries are undisclosed. Operating firms may sit under holding structures in different countries. Shareholder pacts, veto rights, or internal protocols can quietly override what the public record seems to suggest. And in many systems, disclosure is not continuous; it can be partial, delayed, or triggered only under specific conditions.

Transparency is not resisted. It is managed. It arrives on time, in the right form, and never beyond what the law requires. The strategist does not avoid visibility. They design it with the same care they design power—lawfully, deliberately, and with precision.

Designing for Control Without Exposure

Silent Power is not built on hiding, but on structuring influence without attribution. Disappearing is not the point. The point is to direct outcomes without being named, to set direction without leaving fingerprints. Law itself recognizes that ownership, control, and benefit are distinct. The strategist simply leverages those distinctions.

Ownership is what appears in contracts or registries. Control is the ability to steer decisions, allocate resources, or define strategy. Benefit is the enjoyment of value—dividends, access, or long-term security. These dimensions need not belong to one person. In advanced systems, they almost never do.

A family office might record a holding company in the name of a foundation, while control rests with a private council and benefits are distributed according to internal protocols. An entrepreneur may resign as director yet retain decisive influence through voting pacts or irrevocable mandates. An investor might never appear in filings, but issue enforceable instructions to trustees or fiduciaries.

None of this is illicit. It is governance refined. By separating title from authority and benefit from appearance, the strategist achieves compliance and silence at once. Public records fulfill the law, while private instruments encode the true architecture.

Legal Distance Through Structure: Ownership vs. Control

Most legal systems accept that control and ownership are not the same. Many of their most sophisticated vehicles exist precisely to preserve that separation.

In a trust, a settlor may hold no listed role, yet retain influence through a protector position. In a foundation, a council governs under internal statutes, while beneficiaries exercise no legal authority. In companies, shareholders hold equity, but directors run operations—directors who themselves can be instructed through private contracts. A power of attorney can transfer decision-making capacity without conferring any visible role.

This distance creates flexibility and resilience. It reduces liability, avoids personal exposure, and allows continuity across jurisdictions or generations. Above all, it enables influence to operate without becoming visible. Far from being a loophole, it is the foundation of modern governance—embedded in trust law, corporate structures, and institutional practice worldwide.

Proxy Voting, Silent Mandates, and Layered Governance

Real control is rarely exercised in plain view. It lives in procedures, not in signatures. The strategist does not need a seat at the table; they design the rules by which the table functions.

Proxy voting agreements allow others to cast ballots in line with predefined instructions. Mandate contracts place individuals in official roles while strategy is set elsewhere. Side letters may grant veto rights or require prior consent without conferring title. Tiered structures can oblige boards to seek approval from upstream entities—a foundation, a family council, or a private holding company—before acting.

These devices ensure that control is exercised without official presence. Influence flows through agreements, not appearances. Authority resides not in names but in the architecture that frames what names can or cannot do.

Invisible Steering: How Real Influence Operates Under Formality

Some of the most powerful figures on earth hold no public office and appear in no registry. Their presence is felt not through visibility, but through structure.

They steer capital allocation through councils or informal boards. They shape governance through statutes, internal charters, or letters of wishes. They control liquidity through discretionary mandates. They exercise veto powers that never appear on paper but define the scope of action for boards and managers.

A philanthropist may direct a billion-dollar foundation by issuing instructions to its chair, without holding any title. An investor may manage a network of vehicles through a holding company that acts only on private directives. A founder who has stepped down may still shape every decision through an enduring power of attorney.

This is not informal influence. It is structured control—engineered, lawful, and invisible.

Jurisdictional Layering as Risk Management

To keep control both legal and resilient, structures are layered across jurisdictions, with each part chosen for a specific function.

Incorporation may occur in Luxembourg or the UK for reputation and flexibility. Control instruments may be anchored in Switzerland or Singapore, where powers of attorney or proxy agreements are enforceable and discreet. Assets may sit in Liechtenstein or Monaco, where property rights and privacy are strong. Disputes may be directed to neutral venues such as Sweden or ICC arbitration in Paris. Meanwhile, the strategist's personal residence is detached from all of these, preventing it from becoming a point of legal exposure.

This distribution creates a geometry of protection. No single jurisdiction holds the entire picture. Any challenge is slowed, fragmented, or redirected by design. Disclosure rules, scattered across systems, fail to aggregate into visibility.

Here, risk is not denied. It is segmented. Control is not hidden. It is dispersed with precision.

Visibility Thresholds and Legal Arbitrage

One of the most overlooked yet decisive instruments of silent strategy is the intelligent use of visibility thresholds. Every legal system, however strict, is built on limits—numerical, procedural, or functional—that determine when disclosure becomes mandatory. Tax codes, banking laws, corporate governance rules, and compliance regimes all operate through such thresholds. To the casual observer, they appear as mere technicalities. For the strategist, they are borders of sovereignty.

The principle is simple. If a shareholding remains just below a statutory limit—often 25 percent in beneficial ownership registers—no personal disclosure is triggered. If assets are distributed across several entities in different jurisdictions, no single authority sees the whole. If transactions remain under reportable thresholds, they do not automatically enter global transparency networks. Within these parameters, the strategist can engage fully in ownership, financing, and governance, while avoiding unnecessary visibility.

This is not evasion. It is the art of working inside the categories that the law itself defines. Legal systems do not demand total exposure.

They require compliance within their own limits. The silent operator respects those limits but never crosses them unless necessary.

When thresholds are combined with jurisdictional arbitrage, their force multiplies. Every country sets disclosure in its own way: what is mandatory in one place may remain private in another. By distributing entities across complementary regimes, no single authority ever assembles the full design. A foundation in Liechtenstein, a holding in Luxembourg, banking in Switzerland, and residence in the UAE may each reveal something, but none delivers a complete map.

What looks fragmented is deliberate. What appears partial is protective. Compliance is real, yet exposure is minimized. Silent Power thrives not by breaking the law, but by mastering the lines it draws—and ensuring sovereignty is preserved just before visibility begins.

How "Significant Influence" Is Defined Across Systems

Regulators speak of "significant influence," but its meaning shifts across jurisdictions. Under EU Anti-Money Laundering rules, a beneficial owner is usually anyone holding 25 percent or more of equity or control. In the United States, FATCA obliges foreign financial institutions to report accounts linked to U.S. persons who exercise meaningful control—though what counts as "meaningful" often depends on context. The OECD's Common Reporting Standard requires banks to identify controlling persons of passive entities, but only when the roles are clear and formal.

Corporate law adds further thresholds: 10 percent may allow a shareholder to call meetings, 25 or 33 percent may block special resolutions, 50 percent ensures control, and 75 percent can grant sweeping powers depending on the form of the entity. Auditors, too, apply materiality tests, often flagging holdings above 20 percent.

By mapping these variations, the strategist can design influence that avoids triggering unwanted declarations. UBO filings can be sidestepped by staying below reportable percentages. Voting rights may be held indirectly, without crossing formal control blocks. Authority can be diffused across mandates, proxies, or tiered entities. Even tax liability can be shifted or deferred by remaining under the thresholds that activate reporting.

In this landscape, the art lies not only in knowing where visibility starts, but also in knowing where it does not.

Playing Below Thresholds: 25%, 10%, and Silent Capital

Owning 24.9 percent is not the same as owning 25. That fraction often decides whether a name appears in a register. In finance, holding less than 10 percent may spare an investor from deeper scrutiny. These numbers are not arbitrary. They are deliberate lines dividing visibility from silence.

Silent capital can be structured to provide funding, influence, and profit without creating a formal profile. Ownership can be dispersed among fiduciaries or associates, each staying under reporting levels. Economic benefit may flow through non-voting shares, granting dividends without control. Convertible loans or options can defer influence until after a reporting period closes. Limited partnerships may keep minority investors invisible so long as they remain under statutory thresholds. And contracts—granting veto rights, reserved seats, or priority in capital events—can secure authority without triggering disclosure.

The strategist does not need to vanish completely. They only need to remain just under the line where systems begin to see.

Cross-Referencing Across Systems: How Exposure Propagates

Exposure seldom comes from a single filing. It arises when fragments from different systems are connected. Picture an individual who owns 26 percent of a company in one jurisdiction. That company controls 51 percent of a second firm in another country. The same individual appears as a director of a third entity elsewhere. Viewed separately, none of these data points is decisive. But once regulators, banks, or investigators begin cross-referencing databases, the pattern of control emerges.

This triangulation is no longer speculative. Automatic information exchange under CRS, due-diligence routines in banks, and compliance filters for politically exposed persons are standard. Add to this investigative journalism projects like the Pandora Papers, or AI-driven mapping tools now used by regulators, and the risk compounds.

For the strategist, remaining below thresholds is not enough. Discipline must extend to jurisdictional distribution, naming conventions, and behavioral consistency. Without these, the system can assemble fragments into a coherent whole. What seemed discreet becomes legible.

In Silent Power, thresholds are not shelters in themselves. They are only effective when combined with layered jurisdictions and impeccable discipline. Otherwise, discretion is just a puzzle waiting to be solved.

Designing Legal Presence to Resist Triangulation

To avoid being mapped through regulatory triangulation, the strategist must dismantle the chain of inference that systems use to reconstruct control. This begins by separating ownership, management, and personal residence across distinct jurisdictions. When each function is governed by a different legal system, no single authority can assemble the entire picture without extensive international cooperation.

Names, addresses, and digital identifiers should never repeat across entities. Each layer must stand as its own legal node, free of obvious ties to the others. A beneficial owner should not also serve as director, nor as signatory. Reporting trails must likewise be segmented: one entity may trigger CRS disclosures, another FATCA, but neither should lead directly to a shared hub of control.

This separation is reinforced by intermediaries–independent boards, protectors, or autonomous foundations–that absorb operational visibility while maintaining strategic distance. The outcome is a buffered design in which every element looks lawful, limited, and self-contained.

No registry, no audit, no single document reveals the complete system. For investigators to reach it, they would need rare levels of coordination across borders and disciplines. Compliance remains intact, but visibility is fragmented by intent. The goal is not concealment, but the refusal to let presence collapse into a single identity. In an age built on data consolidation, resilience lies in structural dispersion.

The Role of Documentation and Narrative

Silent structures endure not simply because they comply with law, but because their story holds together. Legality by itself is fragile.

Coherence—the consistency of documents, records, and logic—is what makes a structure withstand scrutiny.

Today's regulators, auditors, and journalists do not stop at surface compliance. They examine context, searching for contradictions and implausibility. A trust may be perfectly valid on paper, a foundation may follow every statute, a company may file on time. Yet if the documentation feels incoherent, suspicion follows. And suspicion alone can trigger deeper probes or reputational harm.

The strategist sees paperwork as narrative. Mandates, minutes, resolutions, and letters of wishes are not just formalities. They form a story that must be consistent, credible, and resistant to misinterpretation. The visible fragments should fit together naturally within the legal framework, even if the deeper logic is more sophisticated than the surface suggests.

This does not mean offering more disclosure than required. It means ensuring that what is disclosed cannot be dismantled by inconsistency. A clean, coherent trail is harder to attack than a complex one filled with contradictions. In the world of silent power, narrative discipline is as important as legal design.

Aligning Public Disclosures with Internal Agreements

Nothing compromises discretion faster than misalignment between what is filed publicly and what exists privately. If registry entries diverge from shareholder agreements, or if a director appears independent while in fact operating under a silent power of attorney, exposure becomes inevitable. Courts and tax agencies treat such discrepancies as red flags, often reclassifying structures or challenging their legitimacy.

The strategist prevents this by aligning all layers: registries reflect the same logic as internal agreements; statutes of foundations match the protocols of family governance; board minutes confirm what corporate filings show. Powers of attorney, shareholder pacts, and mandates must reinforce, not contradict, the roles displayed on paper.

When public and private documents tell the same story, suspicion has no foothold. Silence does not come from withholding. It comes from consistency.

Writing the Story That Your Records Will Tell

Every system communicates a narrative, whether intended or not. Regulators and journalists reconstruct that narrative by piecing together filings, contracts, and operational behavior. They ask who benefits, who decides, and whether the design aligns with law or abuses it.

For the strategist, this means the narrative must be authored deliberately. Each entity needs a clear, lawful purpose reflected in its statutes and agreements. Documents must be written with foresight, bearing in mind future scrutiny. Ambiguous clauses are avoided, because ambiguity can be reinterpreted or weaponized under pressure.

Fallback explanations should be prepared in advance: simple, accurate, and strategically neutral. The most convincing story is not dramatic but ordinary—legally sound, logically consistent, and unprovocative. The objective is not to impress. It is to endure.

Managing Inconsistencies Between Filings and Control

Over time, even well-crafted structures accumulate inconsistencies. Ownership changes may not appear uniformly across registries. Informal instructions—emails, side letters, verbal agreements—may drift away from official records. Translations across jurisdictions may diverge, and outdated drafts may circulate long after reforms.

Such gaps create legal friction. Regulators presume concealment, banks freeze accounts, and courts pierce veils that should have been secure. To prevent this, the strategist performs regular reconciliations: annual reviews of public filings, systematic checks of private agreements, and tight version control to eliminate obsolete documents.

A clean system is harder to question. The fewer contradictions, the fewer opportunities for outsiders to pry.

Preparing for Audits, Inquiries, and Legal Mapping

Scrutiny is inevitable. What separates the vulnerable from the resilient is preparation. Silent operators curate audit-ready folders containing only the documents strictly required—nothing more. Drafts for voluntary disclosures are pre-redacted, approved by counsel, and kept ready. Narratives are rehearsed: lawful, consistent, and audience-specific.

Legal privilege is woven into the process so that strategy discussions remain shielded from use in proceedings. The aim is not to conceal, but to control how information flows—making sure that when questions arrive, answers are already prepared.

Confusion, not illegality, is often what triggers escalation. A disorganized paper trail signals weakness. A coherent one deflects attention.

Final Note - Visibility Is a Tool, Not a Threat

The strategist does not fear being named. They fear being understood.

Visibility, handled with precision, becomes a buffer. It fulfills obligations without exposing design. It satisfies without surrendering. The task is not to vanish, but to shape every surface—legal, digital, operational—so that what appears is complete enough for compliance, yet never complete enough to compromise sovereignty.

CHAPTER VII - ASSET PLACEMENT AND SILENT MOBILITY

Ownership Is Not Power—Placement Is

Possession and control are not the same thing, and neither guarantees protection. Within the logic of Silent Power, the real question is never who holds the title, but how the title is positioned, structured, and shielded.

A villa recorded under your personal name is not an achievement. It is an exposed target, vulnerable to taxation, litigation, or political pressure. A yacht tied to a tax-transparent company is not freedom at sea, but a compliance risk that invites cross-border scrutiny. An art collection displayed within your own jurisdiction may win cultural prestige, yet it also risks being swept into disclosure rules, inheritance battles, or even confiscation.

Asset placement, therefore, is not a technical afterthought. It is a geopolitical act. Each jurisdiction brings its own treaties, disclosure systems, and vulnerabilities. By deliberately dispersing holdings across legal environments that do not speak the same language, the strategist does more than diversify risk. They create a fortress of silence—an architecture where no authority can assemble the full picture of ownership and benefit.

This chapter explores how property, art, cash reserves, private equity, and mobile assets can be organized to preserve their usefulness while avoiding unnecessary exposure. It examines the use of corporate vehicles, foundations, freeports, and special-purpose entities as protective layers—each selected to exploit jurisdictional strengths and mismatches. It also considers the discipline of silent mobility: the capacity to move people and capital across borders without triggering tax residence, regulatory claims, or geopolitical leverage.

The lesson is simple. Wealth is not defined by what you hold, but by where and how you place it. Freedom is not measured by movement itself, but by the ability to move without consequence.

Strategic Real Estate Ownership Without Personal Exposure

Real estate speaks louder than almost any other asset. It is fixed, registered, and in many countries searchable by anyone—from regulators to journalists. Bills, mortgages, and insurance contracts often carry the owner's name, tax ID, and address. For the strategist, direct ownership is rarely neutral. It generates legal, fiscal, reputational, and physical exposure.

The objective is not to avoid property altogether, but to configure ownership so that identity is shielded, liability isolated, and registries remain strategically harmless.

Why Direct Ownership Creates Visibility and Risk

Registering property in your personal name guarantees exposure on several fronts. Public land registries often allow searches by name, linking you instantly to a parcel or building. Litigants and reporters alike can tie assets to your identity, turning property into leverage.

The risks extend beyond reputation. Fiscal systems automatically link ownership to obligations: utility accounts, local taxes, and payment flows can trigger reporting under CRS or provide evidence of residence. A property in your name is also a ready asset for seizure in case of lawsuits, even if unrelated to the dispute at hand.

Time spent in the property adds further weight. Courts or tax agencies may treat repeated presence as proof of habitual abode, supporting claims of residence and liability. Even when local protections exist—such as exemptions against seizure—the fact that your name sits on the title already undermines discretion.

In Silent Power, the principle is clear: once your name appears on the title, the design has already failed.

Holding Real Estate Through Layered Legal Vehicles

The strongest defense against this exposure is structural distance. Instead of holding directly, the property is vested in a dedicated company—often a single-asset vehicle such as an SL in Spain or an SA in Switzerland—created solely for ownership and management of that property.

That company, in turn, is held by a higher layer: a foundation, SPF, or foreign holding domiciled in a jurisdiction built for discretion, such as Luxembourg, Liechtenstein, or Panama. Fiduciaries or nominee shareholders may occupy visible roles, ensuring that the strategist's name never appears in public registers. At the top, private mandates or letters of wishes define ultimate control and benefit, invisible to outsiders yet fully enforceable.

Use is then arranged through lawful contracts: the strategist leases the property from the entity, enjoying access without public ownership.

The effect is powerful: the strategist lives in or uses the property, yet litigation risk is insulated, inheritance planning is simplified, and public visibility is removed. The essence of the method is simple—own the access, not the title.

Leaseback, Usufruct, and Decoupled Enjoyment

Control does not require legal ownership. Several mechanisms allow the strategist to benefit from property without appearing in registries.

A usufruct grants lawful use and enjoyment without conferring ownership, keeping obligations tied to the holding entity. Leaseback contracts permit use under market terms while maintaining the entity as owner. In civil law jurisdictions, a commodatum—or loan for use—permits occupation without compensation and without creating taxable ownership.

Trusts offer another layer: the trustee holds title, while the settlor or beneficiary enjoys residence rights under private arrangements that never enter public record.

These instruments separate ownership from enjoyment, protecting against tax residence claims, inheritance disputes, or unwanted association between visible luxury property and personal wealth. The strategist gains control and utility—without leaving a signal.

Navigating Land Registries, Tax Triggers, and Local Compliance

Even the most carefully built structure can be undone by poor execution on the ground. Local exposure rarely comes from design—it comes from operational errors. A single personal name on a land registry entry, a notarial deed, or even a power of attorney can pierce an otherwise silent architecture.

The rule is simple: no detail is too small. Utility bills should never be in personal names. They must be issued to the holding entity or routed through a professional provider. Property taxes must be paid from the entity's corporate account, not from a personal account that links the strategist directly to the property.

In jurisdictions such as Spain or Italy, additional reporting obligations apply to foreign-owned property. These filings must be handled with absolute precision, leaving no space for incidental disclosure. Local agents and managers are not informal helpers—they are buffers. They must be appointed formally, bound by confidentiality, and managed under clear contractual instructions.

Continuity also matters. Who assumes control if the strategist dies or becomes incapacitated? How can the property be sold or transferred without exposing the chain? Does the structure comply with today's substance rules, and will it withstand anti-abuse scrutiny if tested in court?

Owning real estate discreetly is never passive. It is an active design that must be maintained and reinforced against friction at every step.

Silent Holdings in Art, Gold, and Tangible Assets

Certain assets lend themselves naturally to discretion. Fine art, bullion, rare collectibles, and luxury items are not automatically embedded in financial reporting systems. They do not pass through the banking infrastructure that feeds compliance databases, and they often sit outside the frameworks designed for liquid capital.

For the strategist, these qualities make them invaluable. Their power, however, does not come from locking them in a vault and forgetting about them. It comes from placing and structuring them carefully, so that custody and jurisdiction serve as shields rather than liabilities.

A painting stored in a Geneva or Luxembourg freeport remains legally recognized yet fiscally neutral. Gold held through a numbered account can shift between vaults across borders without passing through a personal bank statement. Rare watches, manuscripts, or collectible cars can be insured and safeguarded through entities that hold legal title, while the beneficiary never appears in public documentation.

The goal is not to hide. It is to position assets in environments where the law itself does not require visibility. When held correctly, these assets are compliant yet untraceable, resistant to consolidation by regulators or opportunists. In an age where digital wealth is profiled relentlessly, tangible assets remain one of the last arenas where value can be preserved without noise.

The Appeal of Non-Financial, Mobile Assets

Tangible assets carry three unique advantages that distinguish them from securities or digital holdings.

First, they are naturally detached from identity. A bar of gold bears no registry. A vintage watch does not appear in any international database unless deliberately catalogued. Unless insured or exhibited in personal name, such assets remain structurally invisible.

Second, they can move quietly. Transfers may occur through bills of sale, vault transfers, or private pledges, all outside of mainstream banking pipelines. In these exchanges, documents of title and custody receipts replace electronic ledgers as carriers of value, allowing wealth to cross borders and generations with minimal visibility.

Third, they are versatile. A work of art or a bullion reserve can be pledged as collateral, integrated into private credit arrangements, or leveraged for discreet liquidity. Properly managed, these assets are not static—they are dynamic instruments of sovereignty.

These strengths, however, demand rigor. Provenance, custody, and authenticity must be curated meticulously. A missing certificate or a broken chain of custody can transform a stronghold into a liability. The strategist treats tangible assets not as luxury items but as mobile instruments of wealth preservation—silent, yet indisputable when tested.

Storage in Freeports and Bonded Warehouses

The decisive question is not what to acquire, but where to place it. In this context, geography is law. The choice of custody determines which authorities have reach, which taxes may apply, and how visible the asset becomes.

Freeports such as those in Geneva, Singapore, Luxembourg, or Monaco embody this logic. Technically outside the customs territory of the host state, they allow indefinite storage without triggering import duties or VAT. Inside, art, manuscripts, bullion, and even wine collections remain under customs supervision but outside most domestic registries. Assets remain in transit, legally neutral, and shielded by both physical and jurisdictional protections.

Bonded warehouses offer similar discretion, often enhanced by numbered accounts and fiduciary custody. Assets are tied to codes, not names, with access governed by contracts rather than personal signatures. Such arrangements permit pledging or transferring value without altering the chain of ownership.

Tax advantages add another layer: duties or VAT apply only when items leave the facility and enter the domestic market. Until then, assets enjoy fiscal deferral and discretion.

Not all facilities are equal. Some freeports face mounting transparency pressures, while others continue to uphold robust confidentiality. For this reason, the strategist ensures assets are held by entities or fiduciaries, never directly in personal name. Contracts define who may move or release them; registries do not.

A freeport, therefore, is not just a warehouse. It is a firewall—a jurisdictional shield that keeps value compliant yet structurally beyond unnecessary reach.

Legal Custody vs. Economic Control

The core principle of discretion in asset management is separation: the divide between who holds, who owns, and who controls.

Custody can sit with one institution, legal ownership with another, while real authority remains elsewhere. This deliberate fragmentation allows assets to function fully while keeping the strategist outside the line of sight.

A gallery may house a collection, a bonded warehouse may store bullion, a custodian may safeguard manuscripts. Yet the contracts name not the individual, but a trust, a foundation, a family partnership, or a special purpose company. On the surface, those entities are the owners. Behind them, authority is exercised through mandates, agreements, or letters of wishes—documents enforceable under law but absent from public registers.

This design shifts power from names to instruments. When a painting is loaned to a museum or a vault releases bullion, the paperwork shows only the entity. Even valuations and insurance contracts can be written to reflect structures, not individuals. Unless disclosure is legally unavoidable, the strategist never appears in the chain.

The outcome is quiet elegance: the asset is used, pledged, insured, or sold, yet attribution remains absent. Custodians preserve, entities hold, but direction flows from design. Silent wealth rests not in secrecy, but in architecture—function without exposure, permanence without liability.

Documentation, Insurance, and Discreet Liquidation

Discretion demands more than structures. It requires flawless documentation. Titles of ownership, authenticity certificates, storage agreements, and internal resolutions must be prepared in advance, ready for scrutiny, never assembled in haste.

Insurance must be drafted with the same care. Policies should cover the entity, not the individual. Where possible, brokers or fiduciaries stand as intermediaries, ensuring that no personal reference is embedded in the policy.

Exit is equally strategic. Selling art or bullion under the wrong banner can undo years of design. Discreet liquidation uses private channels, galleries, or institutional buyers under contracts that route proceeds to neutral jurisdictions through entities, not personal accounts.

In this field, discretion is orchestration. Every clause, signature, and invoice tells a story. The strategist ensures it is always the right one.

Private Equity, Funds, and Non-Listed Investments

Private equity and non-listed holdings offer fertile ground for discretion. Unlike public markets, they lack central registers or searchable records. No ticker tracks participation. No public database lists the names of investors. This absence of visibility, when paired with layered structures, creates a domain where influence, capital growth, and silence coexist.

Yet invisibility is never automatic. It is engineered.

Participating Without Public Trace

Private placements do not broadcast participants, but many compromise themselves by signing term sheets in personal name or allowing publicity in press releases. The silent strategist avoids these traps. Investments flow through entities—foundations, holding companies, or fiduciary vehicles—that carry the legal face of participation.

Influence is exercised through advisory rights, voting clauses, or capital commitments, not through personal seats on boards. The structure appears in all records; the individual does not.

Using SPF, SICAV, LP, or Fund-of-Fund Structures

Each jurisdiction offers vehicles suited for silent participation. In Luxembourg, the SPF allows families to hold assets privately, exempt from certain taxes and with no public shareholder register. SICAVs offer flexible entry and exit and are often used in fund-of-fund strategies.

Limited partnerships in Delaware, Cayman, or the UK protect anonymity for limited partners, while influence is tied to capital rather than visible authority. These vehicles can be stacked: a Liechtenstein foundation may hold a Luxembourg SPF, which in turn participates in LPs across several jurisdictions.

The choice is never about fashion. It is about alignment—matching each tool with the legal and jurisdictional environment that keeps the system unreadable yet compliant.

Exercising Influence Through Side Letters and Capital Mandates

In private equity, real influence is often written in side letters. These confidential agreements grant veto powers, co-investment rights, enhanced reporting, or early redemption—binding in law but invisible to public view. Arbitration clauses, often in neutral jurisdictions, secure enforceability without exposure.

Capital mandates extend this discretion further. The entity invests, but fiduciaries or managers act only under written instruction.

Control remains invisible, authority remains private, and influence is exercised without signatures on public boards.

Timing, Exit Strategies, and Jurisdictional Filters

Discretion in investment is as much about timing as structure. Entry before registration can avoid retrospective identification. Exit before audit cycles or fiscal deadlines prevents unnecessary reporting.

Exit routes must be planned from the beginning. Redemption clauses, capital return paths, and profit distributions are designed to match jurisdictional filters and treaty protections. Proceeds never flow directly to personal accounts; they move through neutral structures that maintain coherence and silence.

Jurisdiction matters throughout. A fund position loses value if the return is wired into a high-surveillance system or if custodians sit under intrusive disclosure regimes. Filters must be applied at every stage so that capital moves, but the architecture remains unreadable.

To invest silently is not to retreat from control. It is to reclaim it—by design, through law, and with precision.

Mobile Assets: Yachts, Jets, and Vehicles of Influence

Few assets combine visibility, symbolism, and risk as intensely as luxury mobility. A yacht in Monaco, a jet waiting in Dubai, or a hypercar photographed in Marbella—all carry signals that extend far beyond their use. These assets move, but in doing so, they leave traces: port logs, customs filings, transponder records, satellite paths. Without structure, they transform wealth into exposure.

The strategist does not reject them. Instead, they reposition them. Properly framed, these instruments provide mobility, prestige, and influence without tying their use to a personal identity or triggering unwanted legal connections.

Holding Through SPVs or Leasing Structures

The first rule is distance. No vessel, jet, or prestige vehicle should appear under an individual's name. Ownership is placed in a special purpose vehicle (SPV), often registered in a favorable jurisdiction and held by a foundation, trust, or fund that remains invisible to public registers.

Leasing adds another layer. The SPV owns the asset and leases it back—either to a company or to the user—under commercial terms. This creates a lawful explanation for presence and usage while separating enjoyment from ownership. Insurance, management, and maintenance flow through the SPV, ensuring every contract reinforces the design rather than undermines it.

Avoiding Residency, Customs, and Registry Traps

Mobile assets can entangle users in tax or regulatory claims. A yacht left too long in Italian or Spanish waters risks being cited as evidence of residence. A jet landing repeatedly in France may raise questions about permanent establishment. Luxury cars circulating in the EU often fall under VAT suspicion.

The countermeasure is jurisdictional detachment. Vessels fly neutral flags such as the Cayman Islands, Malta, or the Marshall Islands. Jets register in San Marino or Aruba. Vehicles operate under export plates, diplomatic conventions, or structured leasing models. The principle is clear: presence must not equal connection, and use must not generate liability.

Mobility Without Nexus

A flag is not decoration—it defines the vessel's legal home, its exposure to enforcement, and the degree of cooperation with outside authorities. A poorly chosen flag invites detention or reputational scrutiny; a carefully chosen one renders the craft functionally untouchable.

Ports and airports are likewise signals. Routine docking or landing in high-surveillance jurisdictions creates patterns of visibility. Strategists rotate destinations, choose jurisdictions carefully, and document every role—captain, crew, maintenance—under the entity, not the individual. Mobility here is choreography, not chance.

Documentation, Crew Management, and Silent Operations

Discretion collapses if paperwork contradicts structure. Every contract—fuel invoices, docking permits, insurance, crew salaries—must flow through the entity. Crew are employed by management companies, not by the user. Communication systems are cleansed of personal identifiers, and navigation devices are configured to avoid unnecessary logging.

Silence does not mean secrecy. It means consistency. A jet or yacht may be visible, but nothing in its trail connects it to the strategist personally. Ownership sits offshore. Use is lawful and contractual. The pattern remains unbroken.

Liquidity, Cash Equivalents, and Financial Placement

Liquidity may seem the safest asset class, but it is also the most exposed. Bank accounts, cash flows, and equivalents form the bloodstream of modern surveillance. Capital that is instantly accessible is also instantly traceable—and easily frozen.

For the silent strategist, discretion in liquidity is not avoidance. It is detachment.

Banking Without Attribution

Personal accounts are liabilities. They attach a name, passport, and tax ID to every movement and fall directly under FATCA, CRS, and local reporting regimes. Silent liquidity is held through entities—foundations, companies, or partnerships—that disclose only what is legally required and nothing more.

Jurisdiction matters. Swiss and Liechtenstein banks, Luxembourg institutions, and select platforms in Singapore or the UAE offer stability and confidentiality, but only when aligned with the broader structure. Convenience never outweighs jurisdictional logic.

Jurisdictional Distribution

No serious strategist concentrates liquidity in one place. Risks are not only financial but political and systemic. Banks freeze assets under reputational pressure or regulatory shifts as quickly as under court orders.

Capital must therefore be distributed across uncorrelated jurisdictions, in multiple currencies, under distinct vehicles. Each custodian sees a part, but none sees the whole. In crisis, this dispersion provides not only resilience but leverage: funds can be rerouted or collateralized without revealing the architecture.

Nominee Accounts, Silent Signatories, and Mandates

The name of the strategist should not appear on account mandates. Fiduciaries, officers, or administrators act as signatories under layered instructions—dual authorization, conditional limits, irrevocable powers. Control flows through documents, not login tokens.

Where still available, nominee arrangements add further insulation. Regulated firms may act as account holders with internal sub-ledgers. Rare though these models are, they remain valid in certain high-trust systems.

Managing FATCA and CRS

Even entity accounts can fall within reporting frameworks. FATCA and CRS oblige banks to identify "controlling persons" of passive entities, but treatment varies. Many active entities, foundations with legitimate purposes, or trusts with discretionary management remain outside automatic exchange.

The strategist focuses on classification. Entities are designed to fit categories that satisfy regulators without generating unnecessary disclosure. Jurisdictions are chosen not only for treaty networks, but for the way they interpret reporting obligations. Some apply narrowly, others reluctantly, and a few preserve exemptions.

Transparency itself is not the threat. Misalignment is. Each disclosure must be consistent, neutral, and isolated, so that no authority can stitch fragments into a coherent map of control.

Final Note - Everything You Own Sends a Signal

Assets are not just possessions; they are statements. A property under personal title is more than shelter—it is a declaration. A bank transfer without structure is not just a payment—it is a data point. A jet on the runway under personal registration is not mobility—it is exposure.

In silent strategy, the question is never whether you own. It is how that ownership is read. Left unstructured, assets betray you. Properly placed, they appear neutral, lawful, and uninformative.

Silent asset placement is not about concealment. It is about orchestration—directing what others see while preserving what matters. To own without exposing, to move without signaling, to enjoy without declaring: this is not evasion. It is sovereignty.

CHAPTER VIII - SILENT BRANDING (FOR FOUNDERS & LEADERS)

Introduction: Presence Without Performance

We live in an era where visibility is treated as currency. Founders are expected to step into the role of public figures, consultants are told to market themselves before their expertise, and executives are urged to post, speak, and perform as if their credibility depended on a constant stream of appearances. The dominant culture measures authority by noise: how often you show up, how loudly you speak, how many followers you collect. Within such a climate, silence is easily mistaken for irrelevance.

But not all operators wish to perform. Not all leaders are willing to become the product. And not every strategist accepts that recognition must be purchased at the cost of discretion. Real authority does not always demand spectacle. It can be exercised quietly, through measured presence and carefully designed influence.

This is the practice of silent branding: projecting competence, earning trust, and shaping perception without exposing the individual who stands behind the structure. Silent branding is not the same as anonymity. It is curated visibility—enough to establish credibility, but never so much that the architecture of wealth, networks, or private strategy is revealed.

For founders, advisors, and leaders who value both influence and protection, silent branding creates room to operate. It allows them to direct outcomes without living in the glare of constant scrutiny.

The following sections examine how reputation can be designed instead of performed, how ideas circulate without being tied to personal identity, and how opportunities can flow without requiring personal display. It also shows how leaders can step aside, delegate the surface, or vanish altogether—while still controlling the deeper logic and reaping the benefits of influence.

Silent branding is not absence. It is elegance. It is the choice to command authority without dependence on applause, and to maintain sovereignty in a world that equates noise with value.

Presence Without Personhood

In conventional branding, the founder and the brand are inseparable. Their name, face, and story form the selling point. This model works in industries fueled by attention—entertainment, lifestyle, coaching. But in high-stakes fields such as law, finance, diplomacy, or strategic consulting, it becomes a trap. The more visible the person, the more fragile the structure. Visibility creates liability. Absence becomes weakness.

Silent branding breaks this dependency. It detaches the offering from the individual. The strategist becomes present through systems, ideas, and results—not through personal exposure. The brand stands on its own, credible and authoritative, without the founder in the spotlight.

The first shift is conceptual: branding stops being self-promotion. A brand can be precise, disciplined, and compelling without ever referencing the architect. A legal advisory may publish technical papers. A family office may issue policy notes. A consultancy may deliver insights in a collective voice. None of this requires photos, personal essays, or social media confessionals.

Tone becomes decisive. A silent brand does not shout. Its voice is measured. Its materials are clean. Its presence is professional. It speaks in a way that removes the need to explain credentials or justify authority. Clients do not seek personalities—they seek structures that work. Silent branding earns their trust by being exact, consistent, and restrained.

Every element, from logo to website copy to publication style, communicates the same message: *this is serious, this is deliberate, this is not about personality.* And within that restraint, gravity builds. A brand that does not beg for attention eventually commands it—quietly but decisively.

Presence, in this model, is not about being everywhere. It is about being recognized where necessary and absent where silence serves better.

Strategic Voice, Not Personal Story

Modern branding culture places heavy weight on storytelling. Entrepreneurs are told to share their journey, their struggles, their *why.* Vulnerability is marketed as authenticity. Narratives are framed as the ultimate trust-builder.

In strategic environments, this model collapses. When wealth, cross-border structures, or sensitive advisory work are involved, a personal story does not enhance authority—it undermines it. Once credibility is tied to biography, any change in that biography becomes a liability. A shift in personal circumstances, legal standing, or even reputation instantly affects the brand. Narrative dependence is fragility.

Silent branding solves this by replacing personal narrative with strategic voice. The brand does not answer *Who are you?* It answers *What do you solve?* Relevance is established through positioning, not autobiography.

This voice is precise, domain-specific, and architecturally neutral. A consultancy may release white papers, legal briefings, or economic models. A private advisory may define its own terminology and publish under collective authorship. A holding company may present industry insights without attaching them to a single figure. In each case, authority comes from depth, not personality.

Clients in these environments do not look for relatability. They seek judgment, competence, and discretion. Silent branding delivers this by being irrefutably clear, technically correct, and deliberately restrained.

The voice avoids emotional language, casual metaphors, or lifestyle references. It never blends personal life with professional output. Its credibility comes from the discipline of what is said and the precision of what is omitted.

By refusing the cult of personality, the strategist becomes structurally unassailable. There is nothing to expose, no persona to cancel, no story to distort. The work speaks, the results stand, and the individual remains free to evolve or withdraw without destabilizing the brand.

Voice, in this sense, becomes infrastructure. It is designed, maintained, and scalable. It survives beyond the presence of any single individual.

Controlled Appearances and Selective Presence

Total invisibility is neither always possible nor always desirable. At times the strategist must appear—during a negotiation, in a regulatory process, at a closed-door event, or before a demanding client. The task is not to avoid presence but to curate it. Presence must be treated like capital: deployed with intention, managed with precision, and withdrawn when its purpose is served.

A controlled appearance is not a breach of discretion; it is a continuation of it. By showing up on their own terms, the strategist engages without becoming the object of scrutiny. In a culture of constant exposure, selective presence has power. It creates distance, disciplines access, and prevents a brand from being overused or diluted.

Appearances are always functional, never expressive. A keynote may be delivered under the company's banner, not the founder's name. A media quote may reference a role, not a biography. A filing may carry an institutional representative, even if drafted by the strategist themselves. Each appearance is narrow, precise, and stripped of unnecessary personal markers.

This principle extends to digital traces. A LinkedIn profile may exist, but only with minimal information. A photo may circulate, but not alongside personal details. A name may appear in print, but without the narrative embellishments that invite curiosity. Presence exists to serve a purpose, not to display identity.

Selective presence requires protocols. Before accepting an engagement, the strategist asks: Which jurisdiction is involved? Will this record be permanent? Does it imply financial or reputational declarations? What risks does it carry? What advantages can it unlock? Only after answering these questions is presence allowed—and when it is, it appears in controlled form: initials instead of names, proxy representatives instead of personal attendance, or voice-only statements in place of physical presence.

The logic is not fear. It is sovereignty. The strategist decides not only whether to be seen, but how, where, and to what degree. Every appearance is preceded by a single test: *If this recording circulates tomorrow in another context, does it compromise me?* If the answer is no, the strategist remains in command. Presence is never accidental.

From Founders to Ghost Founders

In the conventional model, the founder is inseparable from the brand. They launch it, promote it, and stand as its permanent face. In the early stages, this visibility can even be useful. But as the structure matures, the risks multiply. The brand becomes dependent on one person. Their health, their reputation, their conflicts—any of it can destabilize the system.

The silent strategist designs against this dependency from the beginning. Their goal is not to be the hero of the story, but the architect of a system that survives, grows, and functions without them.

To become a ghost founder is not to disappear. It is to create conditions where presence is optional. The founder no longer signs every statement, attends every meeting, or performs at every event. Instead, they remain embedded in the architecture: veto powers inscribed in governance, mandates written into protocols, strategic authority exercised quietly from behind the curtain.

There are several ways to build this transition. One is delegation: appointing a CEO, a communications head, or a public director who carries the brand into the spotlight. Another is structural withdrawal: placing shares into a trust or foundation, leaving day-to-day management to visible executives, while influence remains preserved in private agreements. Some founders retain legal presence but maintain public silence. Others vanish entirely from documentation, their control encoded only through layered instruments and fiduciary design.

The model is common among legacy families, sovereign funds, and high-end consultancies. It is increasingly necessary for anyone seeking longevity, discretion, and neutrality. A ghost founder does not weaken the brand. They make it antifragile. They turn attention away from personality and toward the structure itself.

To found something is to leave a trace. To ghost it is to ensure that the trace reveals nothing dangerous.

Final Note - Let the Brand Speak, But Not for You

A brand is not a memoir. It is not a confession or a monument to ego. It is an instrument: a signal that allows others to recognize competence, trust delivery, and choose engagement. When built with discipline, a brand does not depend on loyalty to the person behind it. It earns confidence through coherence, clarity, and restraint.

The modern marketplace rewards visibility more than value. Image is amplified even when substance is thin. For this reason, silent branding cannot exist in isolation. It must be paired with systems—marketing, communication, or delegated voices—that carry the message without attaching it to the strategist's private identity. Influence is never about truth alone. It is also about framing, delivery, and perception.

The strategist knows that presence is easily weaponized. A visible face can be misinterpreted, attacked, or distorted. A personal narrative, however authentic, can become leverage for others. Brands tied too closely to names become hostages of those names. But brands that speak through design, through method, and through structure remain independent of personal volatility.

The discipline is clear: let the brand speak—but never let it speak *for* you. Let it attract attention, negotiate trust, and build influence. But never allow it to define your private identity, dictate your movements, or consume your sovereignty. The moment you and your brand become indistinguishable, you have ceased to be the architect. You have become the product.

Silent branding strips away the noise of ego and leaves only architecture. What remains is durable, sovereign, and immune to the cycles of attention.

CHAPTER IX - GLOBAL NAVIGATION STRATEGY

Borders Are Not Barriers—They Are Tools

Maps suggest a world neatly divided by borders, flags, and sovereign institutions. On paper it looks orderly. In reality, power has never respected those lines. It flows across treaties, hides in asymmetries, and thrives in gaps between systems. For the strategist, this fractured landscape is not a source of anxiety—it is a field of options. Borders are not obstacles. They are instruments: safety valves against risk, buffers that absorb shocks, escape routes that preserve mobility, and layers that reinforce resilience.

To operate effectively today is to recognize that geography matters less for territory than for jurisdiction. Silent Power does not tie itself to a single passport, a single tax system, or a single regulator. It learns to move—physically, legally, financially, and structurally. Global navigation is the discipline of managing these layers so that no observer, authority, or adversary can consolidate the full picture. To regulators, you remain compliant. To rivals, you are elusive. To yourself, you remain sovereign.

Movement becomes authorship. The point is not to be everywhere, but to decide deliberately where you exist legally, where you transact, where you hold assets, and where you are seen. Each choice adds insulation, optionality, and freedom. The strategist weaves these strands so that they reinforce one another, never contradict.

This is not about evasion. It is about design. The task is to place residence, presence, assets, and control in alignment with intention—not with the default rules of any one state. Centralization is the enemy of discretion. It concentrates exposure where it can be most easily exploited.

This chapter explores how to build a multi-jurisdictional footprint that preserves privacy, sustains control, and ensures resilience. We begin by distinguishing residence, presence, and exposure. We then look at treaties, legal asymmetries, and structural combinations that allow freedom without contradiction. The lesson is clear: once you distribute the points of control, borders stop being cages. They become tools of sovereignty.

Residency ≠ Control, Presence ≠ Exposure

One of the most persistent mistakes in cross-border life is the assumption that where you sleep is where you are taxed, judged, or regulated. That notion belonged to another era. Today, residency, presence, and exposure are different realities—each triggered by its own rules, each capable of being separated through planning.

Residency is a legal category. It defines where you are registered for immigration, taxation, or social security. Presence is physical: where you spend time, hold meetings, or consume services. Exposure is functional. It measures how far your wealth, identity, or activities can be claimed by a system. They overlap, but they do not need to coincide.

A strategist may be a resident in one country, spend time in several others, yet structure matters so that exposure is fragmented and dispersed. Diplomats have long embodied this logic. Executives base themselves in Dubai or Singapore while controlling vehicles in Switzerland or Luxembourg. Families scatter physically across continents yet remain united through trusts and foundations that transcend geography.

The lesson is that no single state should ever see the whole picture. One country may provide tax neutrality. Another may offer treaty access. A third hosts banking, while a fourth is chosen for family governance. Each fulfills a role, but none consolidates control. This is not avoidance—it is sovereignty. By separating residency, presence, and exposure, the strategist ceases to be the subject of one system and becomes the author of their own.

The Strategic Separation of Legal Ties

Residency, citizenship, tax residence, and management location are often conflated, yet they are independent levers. A person may live in Portugal, hold fiscal residence in the UAE, manage a company from Singapore, and benefit from a Liechtenstein foundation—all legally, all without contradiction. Each tie is contractual. None are inevitable.

Residency does not equal exposure. Presence does not imply ownership. Citizenship does not dictate taxation. The categories only collapse when mismanaged.

The strategist selects ties for their utility. A residence permit offers mobility. A foundation anchors governance. A holding company separates risks. A private account safeguards liquidity. Each element has a role, but none creates total visibility.

Understanding How Presence Creates Unintended Consequences

Legal distinctions matter, but systems still draw inferences from behavior. Extended stays, habitual use of property, active bank accounts, or recurring social ties can trigger presumptions of residence or "center of life" status. These presumptions often require no proof—only lack of contradiction.

Silent operators manage presence intentionally. They do not accumulate days in high-tax jurisdictions without detachment strategies. They avoid registering utilities or conducting personal transactions that build a profile. When presence is required—family visits, health, or business—it is structured: through short stays, leased properties, or arrangements that prevent authorities from inferring tax nexus.

Presence must always be contextualized. If unmanaged, it becomes attachment. If designed, it becomes neutral.

Designing Movement Without Triggering Jurisdictional Obligations

Mobility is only a strength if it does not create legal ties. Many confuse freedom of movement with freedom from obligation. Crossing borders is easy; exiting systems is harder.

Strategists rely on a mobility matrix. They track visa-free routes, time thresholds, bilateral treaties, and enforcement practices. They avoid breaching 183-day rules. They document detachment when exiting. They prevent family, business, or property from anchoring them unintentionally.

Management functions are relocated outside their personal footprint. Stays are planned around reporting cycles. Travel patterns are audited internally so that no single authority can argue for control.

Movement, when left random, produces exposure. When designed, it produces sovereignty.

The Value of Administrative Disconnection

Administrative traces often matter more than physical presence. A person may have left a country years ago, yet remain visible through utility bills, ID renewals, voter rolls, or healthcare accounts. These signals alone can trigger tax reviews, residency presumptions, or requalification audits.

Strategists therefore practice what might be called administrative hygiene. They deactivate national IDs, close unused accounts, and formally notify tax or residency authorities of their exit. Where deregistration is impractical or risky, they interpose legal layers—foundations, holding companies, or even diplomatic statuses—to manage obligations while keeping the individual at a distance.

Disconnection does not mean disappearance. It means alignment. It ensures that exposure reflects intention, and that no state continues to claim you simply because its files were never updated.

The Role of Jurisdictions in Silent Power

A jurisdiction is more than a place on a map. It is a legal language, with its own vocabulary of rights, duties, and instruments. It speaks through laws, treaties, enforcement culture, and disclosure regimes. For the strategist, learning these languages is not optional—it is the basis of discretion and resilience.

The amateur looks only at tax rates. Silent Power does not confuse fiscal savings with sovereignty. True strength lies in complementarity: one jurisdiction excels in foundation law, another in arbitration, a third in banking confidentiality, and a fourth in treaty access. The strategist does not shop randomly for advantages. They compose a legal symphony where each element has its place, and no single authority can dictate the whole.

Complexity alone is fragility. Coherence is what matters. When ownership sits in one country, management in another, custody in a third, and dispute resolution in a fourth, visibility fragments. No authority can consolidate the architecture. This is jurisdictional engineering: building distance without chaos, compliance without surrender.

Through jurisdictional diversity, the strategist gains not only discretion but operational resilience. Political swings in one state, reforms in another, or reputational shocks in a third cannot collapse the structure. Each layer is insulated by its own legal code, and no registry or treaty can assemble a complete picture without cross-border cooperation. Jurisdictions, in this sense, are not obstacles. They are bricks—when stacked with precision, they form walls of sovereignty.

Why Not All Jurisdictions Serve the Same Function

Every country offers something—but never everything. Switzerland provides confidentiality and legal stability but is not always the right stage for public-facing ventures. The UAE offers neutrality and flexibility, yet lacks certain institutional depth. Luxembourg is ideal for holdings but can be overly visible. Singapore is unmatched in fund management and arbitration. Liechtenstein, for dynastic planning, remains in a league of its own.

The strategist accepts this reality. Different jurisdictions serve different roles: one for incorporation, another for management, another for banking, and a different one for succession. This division makes the system harder to trace, harder to attack, and easier to adapt when rules shift.

Using Complementary Systems for Holding, Managing, and Protecting

Power lies in the combination. A holding company in Luxembourg, owned by a Liechtenstein foundation, managed from Switzerland, and banking in Singapore produces a geometry no single state can decode. Each layer has a role; none is arbitrary.

This layering is not exotic. Sovereign funds and legacy families have long used it. What sets the strategist apart is discipline: no unnecessary names, no redundant filings, no casual choices. Complementary systems create friction for outsiders, but clarity inside.

Risk Dispersion Through Legal Incompatibility

Jurisdictions rarely align. What is visible in one remains invisible in another. What must be disclosed in one system may be exempt in another. This incompatibility is a shield.

Intellectual property may sit in a U.S. LLC, with licensing revenue flowing to a Swiss foundation. A Spanish resident who cut ties before triggering exit tax may still direct assets through a Luxembourg SPF. None of these are loopholes—they are structured disconnects.

When rules clash, risk fragments. No regulator, no claimant, no journalist can assemble the whole. Each sees only what falls within its own borders.

Timing, Entry Points, and Layered Operations

Jurisdictions change with time. Incentives open and close, treaties expire, investor programs tighten. The strategist does not follow headlines; they follow cycles.

Entry is selected with purpose. A residence permit may be obtained not for lifestyle, but to create legal separation. A company may be incorporated not for trade, but to anchor treaty access. A structure may be migrated, not liquidated, to preserve continuity.

Operations are layered. A commercial vehicle follows one set of rules, its holding company another, and its governance structure yet another. Each function is insulated by its own shield. The point is not to find a "perfect" jurisdiction. It is to understand what each can do, and to choreograph them so that the whole remains coherent.

Mobility as a Strategic Asset

Mobility is not a lifestyle choice. It is a structural tool. States assume that people are sedentary: tax codes, residency rules, and compliance regimes all depend on this. But mobility—when managed deliberately—dismantles that assumption.

A strategist who moves with intention breaks the automatic link between geography and obligation. A second residence offers access without tax nexus. Short stays create influence without liability. Carefully monitored day counts prevent fiscal capture. Even strict regimes cannot consolidate control if presence is distributed and documented.

Mobility is not about endless travel. It is about authorship. It allows the strategist to choose where to be seen, where to be taxed, and where not to exist at all. It builds resilience against political volatility and leverage in negotiation, since presence and absence themselves become assets to trade.

To live strategically mobile is to treat geography as a menu, not a prison. Residence becomes a choice, presence a tool, and exposure a variable under your command. Mobility is not movement—it is sovereignty in motion.

Moving Without Establishing Nexus

The real danger of mobility is not the act of crossing a border. It is nexus—the invisible cord that ties you to a jurisdiction and gives it the right to claim your income, your assets, or even your personal obligations. Once a nexus is created, cutting it is rarely simple. Some states define it by days spent inside their borders, others by where your family lives, the property you occupy, or the place you are seen to conduct business. The result is always the same: movement interpreted as belonging, and belonging converted into liability.

The strategist treats nexus as both a legal and psychological trap. Mobility is managed with precision. Days in each country are counted and explained. Families are sometimes spread across jurisdictions not to create distance, but to prevent authorities from consolidating ties that suggest residency. Properties are accessed through leases or usage rights, never direct ownership. Professional activity is routed through entities outside the country of presence, so that even local work leaves no fiscal footprint.

This is not improvisation. It is programming. Calendars are legal documents as much as personal ones. Travel is planned according to treaties, visa regimes, and reporting thresholds. Boarding passes, hotel invoices, and residence permits are kept as evidence, forming a coherent narrative against unwanted claims. Without records, presence becomes assumption. With records, presence becomes proof of intent.

Freedom of movement is preserved only when presence is treated as a legal performance rather than a casual routine. Under this logic, geography no longer defines the strategist. The strategist defines geography.

Time Thresholds, 183-Day Rules, and Center-of-Life Presumptions

The 183-day test is well known, but it is rarely decisive. Many tax systems look further: where your spouse lives, where your children study, which property you use most often, or where your business is effectively managed. These factors together create what authorities call your "center of vital interests."

Strategic mobility dismantles those assumptions. A person may spend 100 days in one country, 120 in another, and scatter the remainder across neutral jurisdictions, never giving any state enough ground to claim fiscal control. Business roles are located in countries where the strategist is not present. Travel itineraries are designed to reinforce separation. Even routine signals—IP addresses, SIM cards, bank logins—are aligned to the declared non-residency position.

Weak mobility models invite presumptions. Strong ones dissolve them.

Strategic Relocation and Reputational Management

Mobility shapes not only taxation but reputation. Where you reside sends a message: Monaco often signals tax planning; Switzerland conveys discretion; Portugal's NHR regime suggests transition. Each location speaks its own language, and others interpret it.

Relocation, then, is both a legal move and a symbolic act. It may calm regulators, reposition a profile, or dissolve lingering audits. It can also be used tactically—short-term presence in a treaty state may open doors for fund structuring, visas, or investment pathways.

Reputation does not begin at customs. It begins with the address you choose to declare.

Negotiated Residence and Pre-Immigration Tax Planning

For most, moving to a new country means surrendering to its rules. The state assumes authority over worldwide income, assets, and sometimes even past gains. But some jurisdictions allow negotiation—turning residence from capture into authorship.

Switzerland permits forfait fiscal arrangements, taxing newcomers on living costs rather than global income. The Netherlands offers expat rulings that fix exemptions in advance. Italy caps taxation on foreign income with a flat substitute tax. The United Kingdom allows non-domiciled residents to shield offshore income under the remittance basis.

These regimes are not loopholes. They are frameworks, designed into law, that allow strategists to enter on terms agreed before arrival. Assets can be reorganized ahead of time. Trusts or foundations may be funded before crossing borders. Unrealized gains can be crystallized, isolating them from future taxation. Even simple timing—disposing of assets or shifting ownership months before arrival—can make the difference between continuity and exposure.

Such planning demands foresight. Negotiations must begin long before relocation, often years in advance. Local rules on domicile, substance, and anti-abuse provisions must be studied in detail. Advisors across multiple countries must coordinate so that a move in one place does not trigger liability in another. Done properly, relocation is not reaction but preemption.

Mobility, under this discipline, is not escape. It is authorship. To move silently is to arrive already structured—before any authority can define you on its terms.

Legal Presence Without Personal Risk

In today's world, every serious activity requires formal presence. Companies need directors. Foundations must name representatives. Regulated businesses require officers or licensed agents. For most, this necessity becomes exposure: names in registries, signatures on filings, identities linked to liability. What begins as compliance often turns into vulnerability.

The strategist works differently. They know that presence does not have to equal exposure. The role can be delegated, engineered, or distributed so that the legal system is satisfied while the individual remains insulated. The law demands that someone be listed—it does not demand that it be the architect.

The separation is clear: function is not identity. A director may be a fiduciary acting strictly under mandate. A foundation's representative may be a professional administrator bound by contract. A license holder may be an institutional partner whose role is visible but constrained. Each visible figure becomes a proxy: an interface that meets legal requirements while leaving the strategist unexposed.

This is not concealment—it is design. Through mandates, fiduciaries, and jurisdictional layering, the strategist ensures that registers, contracts, and signatures reflect formality but not control. The system functions, obligations are met, yet the architect remains absent from the spotlight while directing outcomes from a distance.

Structuring Access Without Attachment

The ability to act—signing contracts, opening accounts, representing an entity—does not require being personally bound. Access is built through intermediaries: entities, mandates, or proxies that interface with systems while shielding the individual.

A foundation may own a company. That company contracts through a representative empowered by internal resolutions. A lawyer may hold a power of attorney activated only under strict terms. An officer may execute instructions without knowing the broader architecture. The system sees lawful action. It does not see who designed it.

Director Roles, Licenses, and Authorized Representation

Some systems require names: directors, signatories, license holders. The strategist never assumes these roles personally. They appoint professionals–fiduciary agents, nominee directors, independent board members, or regulated advisors.

Each operates under limits. Mandates are written. Compensation is contractual. Powers are defined through board protocols, co-signature rules, or legal oversight. Even choice of jurisdiction is deliberate. A Swiss fiduciary managing a Luxembourg company within EU-compatible logic is defensible. A mismatch–such as a Panamanian nominee fronting a Swiss vehicle–invites scrutiny. Alignment is as critical as delegation.

Remote Governance and Virtual Command

Remote governance, normalized in recent years, serves the strategist well. Board meetings by video, resolutions signed electronically, and secretarial support from neutral jurisdictions allow management without geographic entrapment.

What matters is evidence: timestamps, digital audit trails, and records proving separation between where decisions are made and where residence lies. Governance becomes borderless. Presence becomes optional. Risk becomes controllable.

Decoupling Signature from Liability

Signatures create liability, but liability can be layered. A contract may bear the name of an officer acting for a company, which itself acts under a trust, which follows a mandate. Each link is clear in law, yet the strategist appears in none.

This requires discipline. No casual replies from personal email. No signatures outside protocol. All communications flow through professional accounts, encrypted channels, or standardized formats. Authority lies not in whose hand signs, but in who decides what is signed, under which rules, and on whose behalf.

Sovereign Logic: Living by Design, Not by Default

Most people inherit exposure by inertia. Citizenship, tax residence, property ownership, even digital ties accumulate without design. Silent strategy rejects this passivity. Life is treated as a system to be configured—residence, assets, communication, family choices—aligned with intention rather than default rules.

Jurisdictions become options, not masters. Law becomes a toolkit, not a fate. Sovereignty begins when you decide which frameworks govern you, instead of allowing geography or habit to decide.

Choosing Your Legal Environment Intentionally

Every jurisdiction speaks a different legal language. Some reward discretion, others flexibility, others control. A strategist selects them as one selects assets: for alignment, durability, and function. Tax is only one criterion. Succession rules, family law, treaty access, dispute culture, and political resilience all matter.

A single mismatch—between a structure and the principles of its jurisdiction—can unravel years of planning. Living by design means ensuring every tie strengthens the architecture rather than contradicting it.

Lifestyle, Infrastructure, and Legal Autonomy

Sovereignty is not isolation. It is coherence. Daily choices—where children study, where medical records are held, where servers are hosted—must not undermine the architecture. Schools in a country where you claim non-residency, or healthcare linked to a national system, can anchor you against your will.

Digital infrastructure matters just as much. Hosting in Switzerland or Iceland is not cosmetic—it ensures that data lives under favorable laws. Travel habits, too, must align. Spending too many nights in the wrong country or signing documents physically where you deny residence can undo entire systems.

Autonomy is achieved when lifestyle mirrors structure—when every visible decision supports the invisible architecture.

Resilience Through Jurisdictional Diversification

No system is stable forever. Tax codes shift, currencies collapse, politics change. The strategist diversifies—not everywhere, but across enough jurisdictions to preserve options. Alternative residencies, fallback asset homes, diverse banking, and multiple passports ensure that shocks in one system do not collapse the whole.

Diversification is not luxury. It is survival.

Navigating the Transition from Citizen to Strategist

Most people move through life as citizens, tied—legally, emotionally, and even unconsciously—to a single state. They assume that nationality defines belonging, that residency fixes taxation, and that visibility is simply the cost of participating in society. They obey rules as though they were natural laws, forgetting that these rules were created for collective management, not for individuals operating across borders, markets, and generations.

The strategist does not need to abandon nationality to reclaim sovereignty. What shifts is not the passport, but the posture. They refuse passivity. They treat systems as instruments to be interpreted, configured, and aligned rather than as cages to be endured. The citizen accepts rules. The strategist uses them.

This change begins within, not outside. It starts with a question that reshapes perception: *If I could design my own legal identity, what would it look like?* From that moment, every dimension of life becomes intentional. Residence is no longer a convenience, but a structural choice. Banking is not simply an account, but a deliberate placement of liquidity within a chosen legal frame. Communication stops being casual and becomes disciplined, carrying influence while leaving no unnecessary trace. Contracts evolve from agreements into coded mechanisms of authority. Governance—whether of companies, foundations, or families—ceases to be paperwork and becomes architecture.

The strategist remains visible, but only on terms they decide. They comply, but only with systems selected deliberately—never with those entered by default. They may appear to belong, but they are not possessed. Presence in any jurisdiction is conditional, deliberate, and reversible.

Living by design is not isolation. It is not exile or paranoia. It is elevation above systems built for the median citizen. The strategist does not resist those systems, nor attempt to break them. They move beyond them, shaping a legal, financial, and personal identity that remains sovereign in a world designed for capture.

Final Note – To Belong Everywhere Is to Be Owned Nowhere

Systems exist to contain. They classify, register, and consolidate. They expect individuals to have fixed points—an address, a bank, a nationality—that allow easy claim of control. For most, this is convenient. For the strategist, it is dangerous.

To belong everywhere is not about detachment. It is about surpassing attachment. It means moving through jurisdictions with purpose, not dependency. It means being acknowledged without being restrained. It means participating without being captured.

The strategist does not fear borders. They chart them, use them, and then transcend them. They no longer think like residents tied to a single home. They think like architects, weaving jurisdictions, roles, and identities into a design where each has function, but none holds supremacy.

This is not escape. It is not a loophole. It is a discipline. A way of perceiving the world not as a fixed nation, but as a matrix of systems arranged to protect freedom.

Once internalized, this perspective alters everything. The strategist no longer asks, *Where do I live?* They ask, *Where do I place my life so that no one place defines it?* That is global sovereignty—not symbolic, but real.

CHAPTER X - THE FINAL LAYER: SILENCE AS LEVERAGE

Silence Isn't Absence—It's Command

Silence is easy to misread. To the hurried, it looks like doubt. To the insecure, surrender. To the noisy, a lack of direction. In strategy, it is none of these. Silence is an instrument—precise as a signature, decisive as a veto. It is the final layer of Silent Power: the element that binds structures, jurisdictions, fiduciaries, and brands into a single, controllable design. Without silence, frameworks leak. Without silence, plans fray. Without silence, architecture collapses into chatter.

Every system tries to pull words out of you. States demand declarations. Regulators expect explanations. Counterparties ask for comfort. Journalists press for quotes. Adversaries manufacture urgency. The strategist turns that appetite against the world. They understand a simple law: the more they say, the more they give away. So they withhold. They let ambiguity do its work. They use delay as a negotiating tool. They allow uncertainty to ripen into leverage.

This is not passivity; it is authorship. Saying less sets the frame in which others must guess, commit, and expose themselves. Silence makes the room talk. The principal need not stand under the lights to direct the scene—the quiet sets the script everyone else ends up following.

This chapter treats silence not as a shield but as force. We'll examine how it creates asymmetry, compels disclosure from others, and turns uncertainty into control. And we'll refine the practice of calibrated quiet: when to be absent, when to wait, and when a single sentence is enough.

Discretion isn't muteness. It is the craft of releasing only what matters—and making sure the meaning outlives the words. Silence is not a void. It is structure. It is the most invisible—and therefore least assailable—form of power.

The Asymmetry of Information Flow

Every deal, dispute, and diligence process is an information exchange. Positions are staked, terms floated, signals sent. But the flow is never equal. Some speak too soon. Others fill silence with concessions. Many mistake volume for advantage. Power belongs not to the loudest voice, but to the hand that controls when and how information moves.

Silence doesn't erase information; it controls it. What is said, when it's said, how it's framed, and to whom—it's all cadence. The operator who releases less forces the other side to infer more. The imbalance that follows—information asymmetry—creates edge. In markets, timing beats commentary. In law, early framing narrows liability. In diplomacy, restraint breeds uncertainty, and uncertainty pushes the other party to over-explain, reassure, and reveal.

Silence here is not deceit. It is discipline. Omissions are chosen. Delays are engineered. A non-answer is a designed space others rush to fill—often with the very details they meant to protect. The result: you know more than you show, and you show less than you must. To bystanders, it looks like patience. In truth, it's architecture. Silence builds asymmetry; asymmetry applies pressure; pressure yields control. The one who speaks rarely—and only on their own clock—draws the boundaries of the entire exchange.

Why Silence Raises Perceived Value

Abundance cheapens. Scarcity concentrates attention. The same rule governs speech. When commentary is constant, it loses weight. When words are rationed, they gain gravity. Silence, used well, makes every appearance carry more value than its length would suggest.

This isn't mystique for its own sake; it's basic economics of attention. The expert who publishes daily dissolves into the feed. Smart, perhaps, but ambient. The strategist who releases a single paper each year—or chooses one quiet room over a dozen stages—lands harder. The silence before and after does the amplification.

Institutions benefit from the same restraint. A family office that never advertises often attracts stronger counterparties than one that floods the market. Absence becomes a filter: only the aligned and disciplined will approach. Scarcity signals confidence. A person who does not need to explain is presumed to be in command.

Silence increases perceived value because it shifts the work to the audience. Others must lean in, ask, interpret. They elevate what is rare. In a world addicted to broadcast, restraint is the clearest indicator of control.

Managing Timing and Access to Information

Information has no power without timing and audience. A fact released early can weaken you; the same fact, introduced at the right moment, can settle an argument. Control the moment and the channel, and you convert data into leverage.

The disciplined operator treats information as a currency with settlement dates. A legal change is digested internally first; only once implications are mapped is it disclosed—if at all. A counterparty's request is not answered on reflex; silence stretches them into overcommitment. Financial updates go out when they will anchor the narrative already chosen, not when curiosity knocks.

Inside the organization, access is tiered. Not everyone sees the same version. Documents travel stripped of metadata or context, segmented so no single person outside the core can reconstruct the whole. Advisors are briefed to perform, not to map the system. Partners get outcomes; methods remain compartmentalized. Even within families, knowledge follows responsibility—not proximity.

The effect is clarity, not chaos. Controlled streams beat uncontrolled floods. Calibrated timing makes others move to your tempo. Layered access builds resilience: a breach reveals a fragment, never the design.

Strategic silence is not about hiding truth. It is about pacing it. The world will learn what you decide it should learn—on your terms, at your speed, in a form that supports the architecture you've built.

Creating Uncertainty to Control Tempo

Certainty accelerates. It gives others confidence to move, consolidate, and strike. Uncertainty slows the field. It creates hesitation, forces second-guessing, and compels adjustment. The strategist uses this dynamic deliberately. Silence is not absence—it is a pause designed to interrupt momentum and reset the rhythm of events.

A regulator may hold back enforcement, waiting for clarification that never comes. A journalist may postpone publication until they can confirm a story, missing the moment when it would have mattered. A counterparty in negotiation may keep revising terms, anticipating a response that remains withheld. None of these outcomes require rebuttal or confrontation. They are achieved through restraint.

By refusing to answer on demand, the strategist acquires what others squander: time. And time is the rarest commodity in any contest. It offers room to prepare, to observe, to let the impatient expose themselves. Silence converts engagement into a one-sided equation—the hurried lose ground, the disciplined preserve command.

Delayed Disclosure and Tactical Ambiguity

Clarity can be costly. It can trap you in a position too soon or hand leverage to the wrong party. The strategist treats disclosure as a matter of timing, not reflex. Ambiguity is deployed not to mislead, but to avoid capture on someone else's schedule.

This ambiguity is controlled non-definition: no confirmation, no denial, no fixed position until the moment is chosen. It keeps doors open and unsettles adversaries who cannot act without certainty.

Disclosure, when it finally comes, arrives only when risks have dissipated, alternatives have collapsed, or the strategist's advantage is secure. In law, this can reverse the trajectory of a case. In diplomacy, it can realign negotiations. In commerce, it can halt competitors before they mobilize.

Silence in this frame is not passivity. It is authorship of tempo. The process moves when, and only when, the strategist decides.

Withholding Clarity as a Negotiation Tool

Clarity narrows options. Once you declare final terms—figures, boundaries, concessions—you restrict your own room to maneuver. The strategist avoids such confinement. Silence is not avoidance; it is leverage.

Every unanswered question becomes an opening. Each pause forces speculation. Each delay compels the other side to reveal more than intended. Requests for numbers are met with deferment. Demands for confirmation are answered procedurally, not substantively. Opponents disclose their priorities long before the strategist commits.

This is not a trick—it is discipline. The strategist commits only when the terrain is visible, the timing favorable, and disclosure reinforces strength. Until then, silence draws out truths that would otherwise remain concealed.

Structuring Communications to Protect Optionality

Once spoken, words cannot be retrieved. Once written, they gain permanence—and permanence can become liability. Every statement, email, or publication creates a precedent that may be interpreted, reframed, or exploited later. The strategist treats communication with the same precision as financial or legal design.

Nothing is definitive unless it must be. Language is drafted with latitude. Contracts allow interpretation. Emails inform without binding. Weighty conversations are filtered through intermediaries, maintaining distance and deniability. Public statements are written as though they may one day be read in court or broadcast widely.

This discipline transforms communication into armor. It prevents contradictions that unravel strategy years later. It shields reputation by avoiding premature commitments. Most importantly, it preserves freedom of movement—because no position was nailed down before it had to be.

When Not Answering Is the Strongest Reply

Sometimes silence outperforms speech. An attack, ignored, collapses under its own weight. A provocation, left unanswered, loses force. A public question, disregarded, fades as attention shifts. In these moments, silence is not weakness—it is dominance.

Not answering becomes its own statement. It signals that the attack lacked relevance, the provocation lacked merit, the inquiry deserved no recognition. The absence of engagement reframes the exchange: the demanding party diminishes, the silent one enlarges.

Silence creates a controlled vacuum. Into it, no new obligation can be forced, no trap laid, no narrative hijacked. Adversaries waste energy against nothing. Observers expect sound but encounter composure. Meanwhile, decisive steps can be taken quietly—legal actions filed, structures adjusted, alliances reinforced. The strategist acts, but without comment. Outcomes emerge without trail.

Authority does not always need to declare itself. Sometimes it is measured by the silence others cannot withstand.

Controlling Narrative Without Being Its Source

Narratives shape perception, and perception shapes outcomes. Yet the strategist does not enter the arena directly. They guide tone, timing, and context from upstream, while remaining outside the frame of attribution.

Letting the Brand Speak

Institutions carry the voice: a consultancy, a foundation, a family office. They release reports, issue statements, or publish insights. The architect stays absent. The message carries institutional gravity, adapts when needed, and withstands challenge without personal exposure.

Orchestrating Through Proxies

At times a voice must speak, but it need not be the strategist's. Proxies—directors, advisors, fiduciaries—deliver the words. Their statements are briefed, aligned, and controlled. Influence flows, attribution does not.

The power of proxies lies in distance. Contradictions can be corrected without personal cost. Narratives can evolve without reputational damage. The public may hear a voice, but it is not the architect's. The design remains invisible, yet it defines the outcome.

Using Silence to Invite Strategic Assumptions

The most refined form of communication is not found in what is said, but in what is withheld. Silence creates a vacuum, and human psychology cannot tolerate a vacuum. Faced with absence, observers rush to fill the space with their own projections. The strategist uses this instinct deliberately, allowing others to construct stories that serve the architecture—without ever needing to confirm them.

A firm that keeps no public-facing records may be read as deliberately discreet, therefore powerful. A figure who remains quiet in meetings may be assumed to be the most senior, their silence mistaken for authority. A company that withholds financials may be judged not as fragile, but so secure that disclosure is unnecessary. In each instance, absence does not erode credibility. It strengthens it through projection.

This is not deception. It is discipline. It is the choice to remain undefined, knowing that others will assign interpretations that tilt toward strength. Silence here is not a void—it is an engine. It turns uncertainty into intrigue, ambiguity into gravity, discretion into perceived dominance.

The strategist does not tell the story. They allow others to tell it for them—and in doing so, they shape not only the content, but the very act of interpretation.

Non-Reactivity as a Form of Domination

In most competitive arenas—politics, finance, litigation, media—decisiveness is equated with speed. Whoever replies first, counters fastest, or issues statements immediately is presumed to be strong. Yet speed often signals weakness. It shows subordination to urgency.

True domination lies in non-reactivity. It is the discipline to absorb pressure without movement, to allow urgency to dissipate without response, and to act only when timing favors advantage. A strategist who remains still under provocation does not appear absent. They appear unshaken. Their refusal to flinch projects a gravity that reactive players cannot match.

Reaction reveals vulnerability. It shows that your position can be moved, your rhythm disrupted, your time dictated by the opposition. Every quick reply concedes that you have been compelled. Non-reactivity denies this. The attack lands in silence. No adjustment. No recognition. No confirmation that it was even noticed.

This is not avoidance. It is authorship of tempo. In high-stakes contexts, the one who does not yield to provocation dictates the rhythm. Non-reactivity is not weakness. It is the clearest demonstration that no one else sets the terms of your movement.

Breaking the Cycle of Provocation and Response

Every public challenge, hostile question, or demand in negotiation is more than inquiry—it is bait. It seeks to force a reaction, to drag the target into a frame where their energy is consumed defending or explaining. Once caught in that cycle, the aggressor owns the narrative.

Most fall into this trap. They answer to clear suspicion, to preserve reputation, to show cooperation. But in doing so, they reinforce the imbalance.

The strategist declines the invitation. They delay responses until urgency expires. They shift questions into procedure. They allow accusations to hang unanswered until their weight evaporates. Silence here is not read as guilt. It is read as indifference to the attack's terms. By refusing to play, the strategist signals: this arena is beneath me.

What cannot provoke cannot control. Once the cycle is broken, the instigator loses momentum. Their words echo without impact. Their urgency collapses. And sovereignty remains with the one who never entered the fight.

Emotional Neutrality in High-Stakes Environments

Non-reactivity is not situational. It is cultivated until it becomes instinct. In courtrooms dense with tension, boardrooms heavy with rivalry, or media storms fueled by outrage, the strategist relies on emotional neutrality both as defense and as weapon.

Neutrality does not mean detachment. It means refusing to be pulled into emotional currents engineered by others. Anger, vanity, fear—these are signals, and signals can be exploited. To remain internally silent, even while externally provoked, is to retain sovereignty at the very moment others surrender it.

The strategist does not need validation in every room. Their words are sparse, their presence deliberate, their silences weighted. The unspoken message is clear: *I am not here to win this moment. I am here to shape the system.*

Such composure unsettles adversaries, who expect a reaction and encounter none. It reassures allies, who read stability where others project agitation. And it reframes confrontation into architecture—because where others see conflict, the strategist sees design.

Turning Silence into Psychological Weight

When silence is consistent, it ceases to resemble hesitation. It gains density. It becomes a presence in itself—an atmosphere that others must adjust to.

Negotiators moderate their tone before speaking. Rivals hesitate, uncertain how their words will resonate in the void. Even allies temper themselves out of respect for the quiet weight surrounding the strategist.

This is the paradox of dominance: the less you signal, the more others reshape their signals around your silence. The fewer words you speak, the more others anticipate and interpret. Silence ceases to be emptiness. It becomes structure—an unseen wall that directs behavior and shapes outcomes.

At its height, silence is no longer absence. It is pressure. It is the certainty of meaning withheld. It transforms discretion into leverage, restraint into authority. And it proves the rule at the core of Silent Power: control belongs not to the loudest, but to the one who no longer needs to speak at all.

The Discipline of the Unsaid

Silence is not only restraint under pressure. It is the deeper discipline of ensuring that certain words, intentions, and decisions never enter the record at all. In law, in business, and in private governance, discretion does not depend on erasure after the fact. It depends on prevention. What is never declared cannot be exposed. What is never transmitted cannot be intercepted. What is never written cannot be turned against you.

The strategist lives by a simple rule: once something is spoken, it can be repeated; once something is written, it can be leaked; once something is formalized, it can be demanded. But what remains unsaid is immune. It cannot be subpoenaed, archived, or reconstructed. It cannot be forced into disclosure, because it never existed in a form that could be seized.

This transforms silence from absence into architecture. It is not passivity. It is design—the deliberate creation of systems, roles, and processes that function without constant commentary or explanation. The most resilient power is not the one documented for others to read. It is the one that works quietly, binding without exposure, effective without proof.

Legal Silence: What Not to Put in Writing (or Audio)

Every word leaves a trace. An email is not an opinion—it is a witness. A draft is not a thought—it is a potential exhibit. Even casual conversations in digital form can resurface, scrutinized and weaponized years later. The strategist does not assume otherwise. They adopt a discipline of legal silence: never writing what should never be read.

This does not mean avoiding records altogether. It means distinguishing sharply between what belongs in formal instruments and what must remain unwritten. Sensitive intent is embedded into governance documents, thresholds, or contractual mechanics—never into casual correspondence. Opinions that could be misconstrued are voiced in private, not sent in a message. Instructions are built into mandates and defined roles, not scattered through emails or chat logs.

Exposure goes beyond words. Metadata—timestamps, device IDs, geolocation—can reveal more than content. A blank header may still confirm presence. A simple calendar invite may still establish nexus. For this reason, silence also means clearing logs, compartmentalizing devices, and relying on encrypted, ephemeral channels only when absolutely necessary. Over time, omission becomes the norm. Restraint becomes habit.

This is not secrecy for its own sake. It is control: control over what can be demanded, extracted, or misinterpreted by those who should never have had access. In its purest form, silence is not what you keep. It is what you never create.

Strategic Silence: When to Vanish from a Process

There are moments when remaining present in a process no longer serves your interests. A negotiation that has already reached its limit, a public exchange turned hostile, or a relationship where power has shifted—all call for the same move. The strategist does not argue or repeat. They withdraw.

This departure is not weakness. It is recognition that silence can achieve what words cannot. By stepping back, the strategist forces others to overextend, to reveal too much, or to falter under their own noise. Silence becomes a mirror, reflecting assumptions that reveal more than any statement would.

In litigation, it may take the form of declining interviews or refusing to dignify accusations. In diplomacy, it may mean leaving the last meeting empty, the absence itself becoming message. In business, it may mean cutting correspondence at the precise moment when more words would only erode leverage. Each of these exits, timed correctly, speaks louder than argument.

This is not retreat. It is confidence in the systems already built—confidence that structures can withstand pressure without constant defense. It is trust in design, not in dialogue.

Ritual Silence: As Identity, Not Tactic

For the strategist who has mastered discretion, silence is no longer a tactic. It becomes part of identity. It shapes posture, tone, and presence. In meetings, they listen first, allowing others to flood the room with words. In planning, they set direction without proclamation. In influence, they act without announcing intent.

Over time, silence itself becomes reputation. Others learn that when they speak, it carries weight. A single remark may be treated with the same gravity as a full speech from another. What is withheld gains more significance than what is expressed. The strategist is defined not by output, but by the rare precision of their interventions.

This is not mysticism. It is structure. It is communication designed to endure rather than to impress. When silence is repeated, ritualized, and expected, it becomes a language of authority. It signals: power does not need performance. It only needs to be exercised—quietly, consistently, without explanation.

Final Note - Power That Speaks Is Power That Can Be Interpreted

Power that feels compelled to explain itself has already ceded ground. Explanation is an appeal for recognition. Power that justifies itself bends to another's frame, making its movement reactive rather than sovereign. And power that speaks too often scatters its weight, every word carrying the risk of contradiction or misreading.

Silent power avoids this erosion. It leaves no trace to be twisted, no phrase to be weaponized, no confession to be exploited. Its strength is not weakness disguised. It is sovereignty expressed through restraint. It acts decisively and effectively, without needing narrative as proof.

The strategist does not persuade. They do not seek approval. They build. They design systems that endure beyond appearances. They shape outcomes while remaining outside the spotlight. They allow others to speculate and interpret while their own position remains untouched.

Every word withheld preserves space. Every delay extends leverage. Every step away from noise reclaims control. Silence here is not the absence of voice. It is the architecture of presence—deliberate, durable, and sovereign.

Because in the end, power that can be fully described can also be contested, reframed, or dismantled. The strongest sovereignty is undeniable yet indescribable—felt, but never fully captured. True power does not vanish, nor does it perform. It waits, it designs, it moves—breaking silence only when silence ceases to be the stronger move.

CLOSING WORDS

The reflections and strategies outlined in this book are anchored in realities that remain current. Yet it would be naïve to believe the landscape will hold steady. The fiscal appetite of governments—particularly in the so-called advanced economies—grows each year. Their focus is not protection but revenue, and this shift drives tighter controls, harsher enforcement, and a steady erosion of individual and institutional privacy.

The trajectory is unmistakable. What is tolerated today will likely be restricted tomorrow. Transparency regimes will widen, reporting obligations will multiply, and exceptions will be closed under the rhetoric of fairness. Major powers are already pressing smaller jurisdictions to dilute their protections, pushing for wider data-sharing frameworks and stricter disclosure rules. The result is a slow but constant erosion of sovereignty, with those who operate across borders facing unprecedented scrutiny.

The evidence is visible everywhere. In Europe, tax residence is now deeply intertwined with automatic information exchange, leaving fewer safe harbors for lawful discretion. In North America, enforcement grows more extraterritorial, designed to capture income and assets regardless of physical presence. In Asia and the Middle East, governments are rolling out digital identity systems that merge taxation, banking, mobility, and healthcare into a single profile. Globally, compliance systems increasingly integrate artificial intelligence, making patterns easier to detect and harder to disguise.

The next five years will not bring relief. Expect wider beneficial ownership registers, stricter application of economic substance rules, and coordinated campaigns that stigmatize discretion as avoidance. Banks will be pressured into serving as extensions of state surveillance. Even philanthropy and charitable vehicles will face suspicion, treated less as instruments of public good than as potential shelters.

This book is not a substitute for professional counsel. Its purpose is to provide perspective—a framework to read the forces shaping the future—and to equip you with intellectual tools to anticipate and adapt. But no two situations are alike. Every structure must be tailored to the specific legal, fiscal, and personal context of the individual or family involved.

Use these pages as a departure point: a source of perspective, questions, and strategic imagination. They can help you identify risks, frame opportunities, and recognize where discretion remains possible. But when it comes to execution, the path must be designed with qualified professionals who understand your jurisdictions, your assets, and your goals.

Silent Power is not about escape. It is about preparation. And in the years ahead, preparation will be the only true form of freedom.

And remember: silence, when designed, becomes structure. And that structure—if built with discipline—does not merely protect you. *It sets you free.*

www.ingramcontent.com/pod-product-compliance
Lightning Source LLC
LaVergne TN
LVHW052305200926
848481LV00002B/467